Working 101

Library of Congress Control Number: 2006910482
CreateSpace Independent Publishing Platform
North Charleston, South Carolina

Working 101

Everything You Need to Know to Be Happy and Successful at Work

Mike Jacobs

2013

Course Content

Dedication

This book is dedicated to all of the hard working men and women of this world who are commonly referred to as "the working class."

Foreword

Go to any bookstore and you will find the shelves filled to capacity with books about management and leadership. Rare, however, is the book that speaks to all workers, managers and non-managers alike, that shows them how they can truly be happy and successful at work no matter who they are and what they do for a living.

Most of us have to work to make a living by working for someone else. As Michael so wisely points out in *Working 101,* there is no shame in that, nor is there any reason not to do a good job. Everyone, he shows us, has the ability to be successful in the workplace. There is hope for us all.

Working 101 is a wonderful reading experience. You will find it to be filled with great information, highly inspirational, funny, honest, revealing, convicting, easy to read, easy to understand, and easy to put into practice.

I believe that Michael is the most qualified person to write this book. He has made it his mission in life to help others to be better workers, and has dedicated considerable time and effort to that end. After more than fifty years of working and researching, he really knows what he's talking about. I'm confident that as you read the book, you will reach the same conclusion.

If you find yourself wanting more from your job, this book will show you exactly how to get it. If you're happy with what you have, it will show you how to keep it. Either way, you're going to be better for having read it.

Mike Jacobs

My advice to you is this—if you're working, read this book; if you have kids who are soon graduating into the workforce, get it for them; and, if you have people working for you, get it for them. It's a must read.

—Patrick Snow, bestselling author of *Creating Your Own Destiny* and *The Affluent Entrepreneur.*

Preface

Every day, I get up and look through the Forbes list of the richest people in America.
If I'm not there, I go to work.—Robert Orben

Every day, I get up and look through the obituaries. If I'm not there, I go to work. I look at it like this—why be disappointed about not being on the one list when I can be overjoyed about not being on the other? But that's just me.

Not that I wouldn't like to be rich. It has its benefits, of course, and as Mason Cooley once said, "Courage, determination, and hard work are all very nice, but not so nice as an oil well in your backyard." Oil in my backyard? Not a chance. Weeds, sure; dog poop, absolutely; oil, no.

So why am I telling you this? I'm telling you because you and I are not so different. Odds are, you haven't struck oil either, and never will. No, you, like me, will be getting up every day and going to work. That's our lot in life. It's who we are and what we do.

We are charter members of a group commonly referred to as "the working class," which according to economics professor Michael Zweig, represents 62% of the labor force, and is comprised of "people who do not have much control of or authority over the pace or content of the work and are not the supervisor or the boss." (I would also include all lower level supervisors and department heads, who have limited authority and limited training.)

That's from Bill O'Reilly's book, Who's Looking Out For You? The book, by the way, got me to thinking about who, if anyone, was looking out for us. In searching for an answer, it became painfully obvious to me that there wasn't anyone really looking out for us. Dr. Robert E. Kelley, in his pioneering research on star performers, in a round about way, reached the same conclusion. He wrote, "Unfortunately, only a handful of people reach their full potential in the workplace. This is not for lack of effort or potential. It is the lack of access to the best information and the key tools." That's because nobody has bothered to give us this information.

If we were managers, it would be a different story. The best information and the key tools are readily available to them through a wide variety of books, tapes, and training programs, and that's okay because they need to have that information. What's not okay is that we need it too, but it's not readily available to us.

Businesses need to be rethinking where they place their emphasis on training. They have to understand that the key to boosting productivity lies in the development of better workers, and as Fredrick Herzberg concluded in his now famous research on motivation, the key to worker productivity lies not with their supervisors, but within the workers themselves.

Working 101 was written to provide you with the best information and the key tools so that you can be happy and successful no matter what job you have, and I can assure you that no matter what job you have, you can be happy and successful.

It was written with the working class in mind, but make no mistake about it, it can benefit anyone who works for a living, including managers. You can be a brand new employee earning minimum wage or the company president, full time or part time, permanent or temporary, blue collar or white collar, union or non-union, butcher or baker, or candlestick maker—if you don't own the company, then you're working for wages, and if you're working for wages, you can benefit from *Working 101*.

As I said earlier, it is our lot in life to work. To work for a living is, however, nothing to be ashamed of, and nothing to be upset about. *Working 101* will help you to do your job well, and when you do your job well, regardless of the job you have, how much you get paid to do it, or who you work for, you can enjoy it, be rewarded for it, and get great satisfaction from it. I can promise you that.

And one more thing—your happiness and your success are your responsibility. You cannot and should not rely on anyone, be it you employer, your boss, or your co-workers, to help you. They may, but then again, they may not.

Regardless of whether or not your boss is helpful, and regardless of what philosophy of the month he or she is excited about, and no matter what the circumstances you happen to find yourself in, you can still be happy and successful at work.

Introduction

"What is *Working 101?*" "How does it work?" "Why does it work?" "How was it developed?" "Why was it developed?" "How can I get the most benefit from it?" "Who the heck is Mike Jacobs?" "Why should I listen to him?" You sure do ask a lot of questions, but I'm glad you asked.

Working 101 is a complete and comprehensive employee training program. It will give you the information you need to be successful at work. From it, you will learn to form the right habits, develop the right skills, and embrace the right values. Its objectives are to provide you with the information you need and inspire you to act on the information provided.

You won't, however, be learning any hard technical skills that might be required to perform specific job tasks. Your boss can teach you that stuff. What you will learn are the ever important basic, soft skills that are required to do any and all jobs well, without which your technical skills would be wasted.

The program is easy to read, easy to understand. You'll find it to be refreshingly simple, practical, and down to earth. It's simple, not because I'm simple, mind you, and not because you're simple either. No, it's simple because the keys to success are simple. And there's no need to complicate things with charts and statistics, big, fancy words or "heartwarming" stories about famous people who made it in spite of great hardships. With *Working 101*, all you get is good old common sense and the plain and simple truth. You don't need anything else, and I certainly don't need to impress you with my vast vocabulary, my command of the English language, or my wealth of knowledge. My purpose is to help you, not to impress you.

The lessons are structured in a format that is user friendly. Each begins with learning objectives, and moves in a logical sequence, showing you what to do, why you should be doing it, the benefits of doing it and the consequences of not doing it, what most workers are doing and why it's wrong, why they're still doing it, and why they should stop. The lessons end with a summary and some assignments for you to do.

It is the program's honesty and simplicity, coupled with its validity that makes it work. Every lesson is built upon a number of working truths that have been revealed to us through experience and research. These truths show us clearly what works for us and what doesn't work, what's good for us and what isn't good, and what is right to do in the workplace and what is not right. It truly gives you a blueprint for success on the job, and to be successful, all you need is a will to succeed and a willingness to follow the blueprint.

The idea for *Working 101* came to me about twenty five years ago. Out of frustration with what my co-workers were doing and a curiosity about why they were doing it, I began wondering about why some workers were successful while others were not; why some looked forward to coming to work while others came to work looking forward to going home; why some worked hard while others hardly worked; why some always finished on time while others never had enough time to finish. I wondered why there were so many dissatisfied, disgruntled, distressed, and disinterested workers, and why every year, there seemed to be more.

So I set out to find some answers. I asked questions, made observations, and did some research. I took what I found, combined it with my own experiences, and analyzed it all. Twenty five years later, I was comfortable enough with what I knew to share it with others.

Sharing it with others was something I wanted to do, and something that needed to be done. There is so much dissatisfaction in the workplace, not only with employees, but with employers as well, who are dissatisfied with their workers. Both, it turns out, are dissatisfied for the very same reason—there are too many workers who lack the basic, soft skills that are necessary for success at work.

We need these skills, but until now, the information we need to help us develop these skills has not been readily available to us. This has forced us to learn as we go, on the job. We can learn from on the job experiences, but they can be painful experiences, to say the least. We can learn the right way to do things, but more often than not, we learn the wrong way. Why? Because in the absence of the best information, we are forced to learn from each other, which is not always a good thing. An old Latin proverb tells us that a wise man learns from the mistakes of others, a fool by his own. However, when we learn from people who don't know what they're doing, and no one is there to correct us, we tend not to learn from their mistakes, but to make the very same mistakes. *Working 101* will allow you to learn from the

Mike Jacobs

mistakes people make without the risk of making them too. Think of it as getting on the job experience from a book.

Now, let's talk about me. Who am I, and what qualifies me to write this program? Why should you believe what I say? Good questions, both, and you deserve to know the answers.

I'm reminded of an ancient Chinese proverb, which says, "To know the road ahead, ask those coming back." Well, after fifty one years of working, ever since my thirteenth birthday, I think I can safely say that I'm "coming back." I've been there and done it all. I've paid my dues, and while doing that, I've paid attention too. I've gained the experiences, asked the questions, did the research, made the observations, and did my best to make sense of it all. If that doesn't qualify me, I don't know what will. It's not like I could have gotten a PhD in workology, because there is no such thing. And it's not like I had to be a genius to write this program, as you probably figured out when I told you it took me twenty five years to write it.

Not that it really matters who I am. What matters is what I have to say. The program is important, not me, and the program works. It works because everything in it is true. I didn't make any of this stuff up. All I did was open my eyes, my ears, and my mind to what was going on around me, and wrote it all down.

And now, I pass on to you what I have learned. It's up to you make of it what you can, to open your eyes, your ears, and your mind, and listen to what I have to say.

To maximize your learning experience, I suggest that you:

- Make it personal. See if you can recognize the behaviors being described as something that you or your co-workers do. Be honest with yourself. I must warn you here that **this book can be hazardous to your ego** because you will see yourself and your co-workers within its pages and not always in a favorable light.
- Take your time reading the book. Stop to think about what is being said.
- Read it more than once.
- Discuss it with your co-workers.
- Do the "homework" assignments in each lesson. (Although no one will be checking your homework.)
- Keep learning from other sources.
- Give it a try. See if it works for you. Then go back to the book and compare your experiences with what the book says.
- Have fun!

Lesson One: Work, and What It Means To You

<u>Objectives:</u>

1. To learn to appreciate work.
2. To understand the benefits of working.
3. To understand how your attitude affects your work.

Do you think of work as a means to better yourself or as a burden or chore, something that you do only because you have to? This is an important question because what you think of it will, to a great extent, determine how well you do at it. Evidence shows that people who like what they're doing, do it well, whereas people who don't like what they're doing, do it poorly. And it works both ways. People who do well, come to like what they're doing, whereas people who do poorly, come to dislike what they're doing.

There is obviously an important connection between job performance and job satisfaction. Look around and see for yourself. The most productive workers are not going to be the ones who are sitting around complaining about their jobs and talking about their plans for the weekend. Productive workers are too busy working.

Mike Jacobs

3D Workers

Job dissatisfaction is widespread in the workplace and spreading all the time. Many workers are what I call "3D workers"—Disgruntled, Dissatisfied, and Disinterested. Several surveys have been done, and without exception, have concluded that job dissatisfaction is a growing concern. But you already know that. As both an employee and a consumer, you see and hear the rudeness, the indifference, and the incompetence all the time, from the waitress who makes it obvious that she's not happy about waiting on one more table to the store clerk who ignores you because he's busy trying to get the new girl to go out with him; from the cashier at the supermarket who rings up the wrong amount because he's not paying attention to the receptionist who disconnects you after you've been on hold for five minutes. It's ridiculous. Everyone's talking about customer service today, but as customers, we have learned not to expect it.

Everywhere you go, you hear workers talking trash about their bosses, their co-workers, their customers, and their jobs. They spend more time talking about what they're going to do after work than thinking about what they should be doing at work. I like to refer to this as the "work sucks syndrome." It's everywhere. You can listen to it at work, turn on your TV or radio, watch a movie, read the paper, or surf the Internet. I guarantee that someone will be trashing work. It's been said so many times by so many people in so many places that we have come to really believe that work does suck.

DID YOU KNOW? In the song, "All The Small Things," by Blink 182, there's a line that goes, "Late night, come home; work sucks, I know."

DID YOU KNOW? There are hundreds of websites on the Internet that are dedicated to trashing work, including, "Worksnotfun.com" and "Jobhaters.com"

Work does not suck. It's the "work sucks syndrome" that sucks. It only serves to foster discontent and resentment towards work. When workers believe that work sucks, for them, it does. The reality is that it's not the work that sucks, but the bad attitudes that workers bring to their jobs.

Work is good, and it is good for you. To live you must work, and by working, you are made better. "Work," said Tolstoi, "is the inevitable condition of life, the true source of human welfare."

The benefits of work

- Gets you money and the things that money can buy.
- Builds character, self confidence, and self esteem.
- Gives you a sense of accomplishment and personal satisfaction.
- Promotes good mental and physical health.
- Allows you the opportunity to be of service to others.
- Gives you an identity and a sense of purpose.

- Provides you with opportunities to socialize and make new friends.
- Helps you to make contacts who can be of assistance to you in the future.
- Gives you the needed experience that employers are looking for.
- Helps you to develop skills and form habits that will serve you later.
- Allows you to know your strengths and weaknesses.
- Meets your biological need to work.
- Gives you something to do.
- Makes you feel like you're part of something big.
- Enables you to be independent.

Some genius once said, "What's so good about work if they have to pay you to do it?" That is what's good about it, that they pay you to do it. Money is not the only benefit to working, and arguably, may not even be the most important benefit. But there's no denying its importance to you. Without it, you would be hard pressed to obtain either the basics you need to live or the luxuries you want to enjoy. A poster we have hanging at work reads, "Working here allows me to enjoy two of the luxuries I have become accustomed to, eating and living indoors."

DID YOU KNOW? There's a quote in the Bible which says, "This we command you, that if any would not work, neither should he eat."

Should work just be about earning a wage? Isn't there more to life than money? We spend a huge portion of our lives at work. Why shouldn't that time be traded for more than just bucks and benefits? Why shouldn't work also be satisfying? Shouldn't we also find a sense of meaning and fulfillment on the job? Why can't we look forward to going to work with as much anticipation as we look forward to weekends, holidays, and vacations?—William Byham

I couldn't agree more, and yes, it is about more than just earning wages and benefits. It's about building character, self confidence, and self esteem. In the words of John Ruskin, "The highest reward for a person's toil is not what they get for it, but what they become by it." And as Paul J. Fleyer suggests, "Good work habits help develop an internal toughness and a self confident attitude that will sustain you through every adversity and temporary discouragement." These are not things you can easily get from standing in the unemployment line!

It's about having a sense of accomplishment and feeling satisfied. "The reward of a thing well done," said Ralph Emerson, "is to have done it." When you've done a good job, and you know it, it makes you feel real good about yourself. When others recognize what you've done, it feels even better still.

It's about feeling good physically and mentally. As John Wanamaker noted, "The healthiest and happiest people in the world are those privileged to work a full business day." Health and happiness are not generally associated with being out of work, with nothing to do and nowhere to go.

It's about being of service to your fellow man. Few things in life bring you greater satisfaction than doing your job well, especially when it is in service to others.

Ralph Emerson wrote, "It is one of the most beautiful compensations of this life that no man can sincerely try to help another without helping himself."

It's about finding an identity and purpose in your life. Who are you? What do you do for a living? That's what everyone wants to know. You are much more than what you do, but what you do is so much of who you are. As Joseph Conrad said, "A man is a worker. If he is not that, he is nothing."

It's about having the opportunity to socialize, to meet new people and make new friends, or to develop contacts who can be of assistance to you now or later. It never hurts to know the right people.

It's about learning new skills and developing new work habits, all of which will serve you throughout your life; about discovering your strengths and uncovering your weaknesses; about finding out what you like to do and what you dislike doing; about gaining the ever valuable experience you need to move on to bigger and better jobs, experience, without which, those jobs would be closed to you forever.

It's about fulfilling your need to work. Hans Selye, the foremost researcher on stress, concluded that work is a biological necessity. Even the famous artist, Picasso, agreed, and suggested that man invented the time clock for this very reason. (Okay, so there is something bad about work.)

It's about having something to do. "Few people," wrote Og Mandino, "realize how much of their happiness is dependent upon their work, upon the fact that they are kept busy and not left to feed upon themselves. I am nothing without my work. The prime secret of happiness is something to do." A French proverb also tells us that "work relieves us from three great evils—boredom, vice, and want."

It's about freedom, to do what you want to do, to get what you want to have, to go where you want to go, to be who you want to be, with or without anyone's help.

That's what work is all about, and you are not its only beneficiary. When you do your work, and do it well, customers benefit, businesses benefit, the economy benefits, the nation benefits, and the whole world benefits.

How could something that does all this for you suck? How could you believe that it does? Take my advice and don't believe it, because when you believe that work sucks, and when you work like you believe it, for you, it will suck. It will suck now and it will suck later on, no matter where you work and no matter how many times you change jobs, because when you have a bad attitude about work, you take it with you everywhere you go.

Get this stupid "work sucks syndrome" out of your head. If you have a job, be thankful that you have it. It's a whole lot better than not having a job. Focus your attention, instead, on doing the best job you can do. Remember these words from Ulysses S. Grant—"Labor disgraces no man, but occasionally men disgrace labor." It is never a disgrace to work, but it is a disgrace to work poorly.

SUMMARY

- Work does not suck.
- To live, we must work; by working, we are made better.
- When you believe that work sucks, it does for you.
- When you like what you're doing, you'll do it better.

- When you're better at what you're doing, you'll like it more.
- Bad attitudes about work follow you wherever you go.

Assignments:

1. Make a list of all the benefits you get from your job. To make it easier, start each one with something like "I became," "I learned how to," "I met," "I felt," "I got," "I did,"…
2. After reviewing your list, answer the question, "does work suck?"
3. If your answer is no, congratulations, you're on your way to success and happiness. If your answer is yes, see #4.
4. Read lesson one again, and answer the questions again.
5. This time, if you can't think of enough benefits to your job, perhaps you should think about finding a new job.

Lesson Two: Your Job, and What It Means To You

<u>Objectives:</u>

1. To appreciate why you should do your job to the best of your ability.
2. To understand that all jobs are important.
3. To learn the four options you have for dealing with a job you don't like.

It's just a job.
Grass grows, birds fly,
waves pound the sand.
I beat people up.—Muhammad Ali

It's not just a job! There's no such thing. Every job is important, to the business that creates it, to the customers who are served by it, and to the workers who work at it.

The company you work for did not create your job just for the hell of it or just to be nice, and it certainly wasn't looking for a way to throw away its money. No, it, like all companies, wants certain things—to be in business, to stay in business, and to succeed in business.

To get what it wants, the company needs:

- Customers (a reason to be in business)
- A Mission (a sense of direction)
- Products or services (a means of obtaining revenues)

- Manpower (to operate the business)
- Information (on which to run the business)
- Money (with which to run the business)
- A plan (on how to run the business)

Jobs are created for a purpose—to meet these needs. Your job may serve one or more of the following purposes:

- To bring in, identify, satisfy, serve, track...<u>customers.</u>
- To envision, write, teach...<u>a mission.</u>
- To develop, build, ship, store, provide...<u>products or services</u>
- To hire, train, pay, assess...<u>manpower.</u>
- To gather, disseminate, document...<u>information.</u>
- To make, save, distribute, count...<u>money.</u>
- To develop, revise, implement...<u>a plan.</u>

It's important that you understand the difference between the things you do at work and the purpose your job serves. To illustrate this point, we'll look at some typical jobs.

Let's say you're a janitor working in a big department store. Your work consists of sweeping, mopping, waxing, vacuuming, etc. That's what you do, but it's not what your purpose is. Your purpose is to keep the store clean, safe, and sanitary, making it a nice place to work and a nice place to shop. When your purpose is served, productivity increases, employee morale improves, accidents and illnesses are reduced, and customers are satisfied. When customers are satisfied, sales increase and complaints are reduced.

If you're a good janitor, you will work tirelessly to ensure that floors are always shiny and spotless, and safe to walk on. You will care about how those floors look, and you'll be proud when they look good, angry at yourself when they don't. You will do this because you understand the purpose of your job.

I tell you this, having seen so many janitors, and housekeepers too, who obviously couldn't care less how the floors looked. I've seen them literally go out of their way to avoid having to clean up a spill, walking around it or stepping over it, and then swearing that they never saw it. What purpose could that possibly serve?

Now let's say that you're working in a fast food restaurant, making hamburgers. You read the orders, cook up the burgers, slap on the condiments, wrap it all up and pass it on to the person taking the orders. That's what you do, but it's not what your purpose is. Your purpose is to ensure that customers are satisfied by giving them exactly what they ordered, cooked properly, and served quickly. When your purpose is served, less food is wasted, customers keep coming back, fewer complaints are made, and fewer burgers are returned by irate customers who get home, sit down to eat, and discover, to their displeasure, that they didn't get what they ordered from those blankety blanks at the fast food place.

If you're a good fast food worker, you will know that in the fast food business, "have it your way...sometimes," is not good enough. If your customers can't get it their way from you, they can get it elsewhere. You don't want that to happen, so you work tirelessly to get it right...every time. You feel proud when customers are happy, angry at yourself when they're not. And this I tell you, having bitten into too many burgers that weren't made the way I wanted them to be made.

I don't want to belabor the point. Your job, whatever it is, serves a purpose, a very important purpose. Serve it well, and when you do, be proud of what you have done. Those are your floors that people are walking on, your burgers that people are eating, so take ownership of the way they're done.

It's a shame that in spite of the purpose that every job serves, there are still so many workers who are ashamed of what they do for a living, so much so for some that they use different titles to refer to their jobs—janitors become building superintendents; salesmen become account executives; garbage collectors become sanitation engineers.

Why? There is absolutely nothing wrong with being a janitor, a salesman, or a garbage collector. There is no reason to be ashamed of any job just because it doesn't come with a fancy title, a big office, or a hefty paycheck. If you're ashamed of your job, if you lack pride in doing it because it doesn't come with any of these things, I have news for you—you're looking for pride in all the wrong places. If there is honor to be found in the workplace, it is not to be found in the jobs themselves, or in the perks that come with the jobs, but in the people who work those jobs.

You can be proud sitting in a big office, sitting in a little cubicle, standing behind a counter, driving in a car, or walking around all day. It makes no difference. You can be proud having a solid gold nameplate on your desk or wearing a plastic nametag on your shirt. It makes no difference. Listen, at sixty four years old, I'm still wearing a nametag, and I'm proud of it, and well paid for it.

History speaks

Every calling is great when greatly pursued.—Oliver Wendell Holmes

No labor, however humble, is dishonoring.—The Talmud

There are no menial jobs, only menial attitudes.—William Bennett

The quality of a person's life is in direct proportion to their commitment to excellence, regardless of their chosen field of endeavor.—Vince Lombardi

If a man is called to be a street sweeper, he should sweep streets as Michelangelo painted, or as Beethoven composed, or as Shakespeare wrote poetry. He should sweep streets so well that all the hosts of heaven will pause to say, here lived a great street sweeper who did his job well.—Dr. Martin Luther King

In case you didn't notice, Dr. King said street sweeper, not road engineer. All of these good folks are trying to tell you that it doesn't matter what you do for a living, only that you are committed to doing it well. People who achieve great success know that this is true. They know, that with few exceptions, those who make it to the top almost always start at or near the bottom, and that every job they have, from the bottom on up, adds something of value that enables them to make it to the top. Early on, they recognize the value of every job they have, so they do their best no matter what the job is.

For you to succeed, you must believe that the job you have, right now, is the most important job you'll ever have. It doesn't matter what your job is, how much you're getting paid to do it, or what anyone else might think about it. It is the most important job you'll ever have, until, of course, your next job. The point is that you must believe that it is, and then behave accordingly. And when you do, all the benefits that come from working will come to you.

The four options

You hate your job. The work is too hard, they don't pay you enough, your boss is a jerk, your co-workers are not helpful, and your customers are not appreciative. Now what? What are your options?

1. You can do nothing different.
2. You can find another job to hate
3. You can find a job that you will love.
4. You can learn to love the job you have.

Option #1: You can do nothing different. You can stay there and continue to be miserable, and probably make everybody around you miserable too. Since you're doing nothing but complain about people and circumstances, people and circumstances will never change.

Option #2: You can find another job to hate. Why not? Many people choose this option. They have no idea what they want to do, so they jump at the chance to work somewhere else as long as it sounds good. They take what they can get, which is usually whatever is left over after all the better jobs have been taken. It doesn't take long before they realize that the grass is not always greener somewhere else, which is, as you already know, because of the baggage they bring with them.

It's easy to see that options one and two are not very good options. This, however, does not stop millions of workers from choosing them. I think there are many reasons for this, not the least of which are low self esteem, laziness, and indecision. Perhaps the biggest reason is that most people are unaware of options three and four.

Option #3: You can find a job that you will love. It's harder to find a job you can love than to just find another job because it's not just about getting out of something you hate, it's also about getting into something you love. It will take some time and patience.

Step One is to stay where you are. Grin and bear it if you must, but stay. It's much harder to find a new job than to keep an old one, and it's much easier to find a new job when you already have a job. Potential employers do not look favorably upon applicants who are out of work. It's like trying to get a loan from your bank. They're not going to give you one until you prove to them that you don't really need it.

Step Two is to decide what kind of work you would like to be doing. What do you believe in? What peaks your interest? What are you good at doing? You need to ask yourself these questions because if you could do what you believe in, you will believe in what you do; if you could do what peaks your interest, you will take interest in what you do; and, if you could do what you are good at doing, you will do it well.

There are lots of good jobs out there, especially for those who know what they want to do, are willing to work at it, and willing, also, to go looking for it. The reality is, however, that most people have no idea what they want, are unwilling to work for it, and unwilling to spend any time looking for it. They're too busy complaining about the jobs they have. It's no wonder they're going nowhere fast.

Step Three is to develop a plan. Know the type of work you want to do, find out where you can get that type of work, what skills you will need, how much experience, if any, will be required, what further education you might need to acquire, how and where you can get the skills, the experience, and the education, and who can help you if you need it.

With respect to education, although most employers understand that an education is no guarantee of success, many still require some. To get the education you need, you don't have to quit your job. You can attend evening classes, take online courses, enroll in home study programs, or read books. Anything you need to know can be found in your local library or on the Internet. Financing is always available for most of these things if you need it.

Getting experience sometimes presents a bit of a dilemma—without experience, some jobs are hard to get, but if you can't get those jobs, how do you ever get the experience? Easy, you offer the employer something other than experience—a positive attitude, a nice appearance, a vision or plan describing how you can contribute to the company's success, an eagerness to learn, or a willingness to start for less money than what they are willing to pay. The idea behind taking less money is to demonstrate your confidence in your abilities and to get your foot in the door. Once in, you can show them what you can do, and earn more. To many employers, these things are worth more than experience. To some employers, a lack of experience is a good thing because it tells them that you will be coming to them with no bad habits or preconceived notions.

Contacts are important too. At work, it's not a matter of who you know or what you know, it's a matter of who and what you know. People can, and will, help you to succeed by serving as mentors, providing references, or putting you in touch with others who can help. If you need help, it never hurts to ask. A word of advice, though—if someone helps you to get a job, don't embarrass them by doing it poorly.

Step Four is to apply for and interview for the job you want, keeping these points in mind:

- Be prepared. Bring a resume, but if you don't have one, bring a list of the jobs you have had, the schools you have attended, the references you are providing, and the dates when you did these things. You want to fill out their application completely, correctly, and neatly. Also, find out what you can about the company you are applying to before you get to the interview.
- Be on time. If you don't make it to the interview on time, why should they believe that you will come to work on time? First impressions are often lasting impressions.
- Stay calm. The interviewer's job is to hire people, not to scare them away. If you're nervous, tell the interviewer that you are, and that it's because you really want the job. He expects you to be nervous, and will appreciate your honesty.
- Be honest on your application and in your interview. Interviewers are often trained to spot inconsistencies. If they spot even one, you won't get the job. If you've made mistakes in

the past, admit them. They'll be more likely to forgive past mistakes than to forgive dishonesty.
- Dress conservatively. Wear nice, clean clothes appropriate to the type of job you are seeking. Leave your nose rings and purple hair dye at home.
- Don't argue. Even if you win the argument, you can still lose the job. While you're at it, don't use certain words that tend to scare employers off, like union, harassment, discrimination, and worker's compensation.
- Think about how you will answer the questions that interviewers almost always ask—why do you want to work here? What do you want to be doing in five years? What is your greatest strength? What is your biggest weakness? What do you think you can bring to this company? Why should we hire you?

DID YOU KNOW? Sometimes, people are too honest on interviews. The following are actual answers given to the questions above:

- Why do you want to work here? Because nobody else will hire me.
- Where do you want to be in five years? Working somewhere else.
- What is your greatest strength? Looking good on interviews.
- What is your biggest weakness? Getting motivated to work.
- What do you think you can bring to this company? Was I supposed to bring something?
- Why should we hire you? Beats me.

Finding a job you can love may take time, effort, and even sacrifice, but it's well worth it. No matter how long it takes you to get there, it will be nice to get there, and nice not to be where you are right now. The journey will be as rewarding as the destination, and it's never too late to start.

Option #4: You can learn to love the job you have. For most workers, this option turns out to be the best option. At the very least, you know what you've got. If you're going somewhere else, you'll never know what you're getting into until after you've already gotten there.

Besides, we already know that if you're having issues at your job now, unless you resolve them, you'll have the same issues wherever you work. Why not, then, stay where you are and resolve your issues now? Staying does have its benefits, including bigger paychecks, longer vacations, more promotions, and the opportunity to be given choice job assignments.

What, you may ask, is all this talk about loving my job? Can't I just do it without loving it? And how can I learn to love a job that I'm miserable at? Well, the short answer is that you don't have to do anything you don't want to do. But I ask you this, wouldn't you rather get up in the morning and go to work at a job you really love than to get up and go to work at a job that makes you miserable?

Confucius said, "If you love your job, you will never have to work a day in your life." Katherine Graham asks, "To love what you do and feel that it matters, how can anything be more fun?" Walter Chrysler adds, "I feel sorry for the person who can't get genuinely excited about his work. Not only will he never be satisfied, but he will never achieve anything worthwhile."

These good people all recognize a simple truth, that if you love what you're doing, you'll have fun doing it, you'll be genuinely excited about it, and you'll be much better at doing it. If you love your job, you'll want to do it, and when you want to do something, you'll do it better than when you're doing it just because you think you have to. Conversely, as you get better at doing your job, you'll begin to love it more and enjoy it more. As Pearl Buck said, "The secret of joy in work is contained in one word, excellence. To know how to do something well is to enjoy it."

The secret of loving your job is, to you, no secret at all. It is to treat your job as though it was the most important job you will ever have. Do this, and never again will you have to wait painfully until the end of the week for the opportunity to say—"Thank God it's Friday."

SUMMARY

- There is no such thing as "just a job."
- Every job is important, to the business that creates it, to the customers who are served by it, and to the people who work at it.
- The job you have right now is the most important job you will ever have…until your next job.
- It's not the job you have that counts, but the job you do.
- If you're not happy with your job, the best option for you is to stay there and learn to love it.

Assignments:

1. Find out what your purpose is at work. Ask your boss; talk to your co-workers; give it some thought. To assist you, ask these questions—"If my job didn't exist, who would be affected by it and what would happen?" "What happens when I do a great job?" "What happens when I do terrible job?" Reread the section in this lesson for more assistance, and if all else fails, contact me through my website www.workingtruths.com.
2. Think about your job. Do you love it, like it, tolerate it, or hate it? If you don't at least like it, look at your four options and decide which one to take.

Lesson Three: Success At Work

1. To adopt a more realistic definition of success.
2. To understand the personal nature of success.
3. To determine your willingness to succeed.

What is success at work? How do you know when you have achieved it? Most workers, if asked, would either have no idea, having never given it any prior thought, or would say it had something to do with having all the perks—a fancy title, a corner office with a window, and a big, fat paycheck. Success, to many workers, is not something that applies to people like them.

What does success mean to you? Why should that matter? It matters what you think because how you define success will help to determine whether or not you achieve it. Timothy Gallwey wrote, "We are used to thinking of definitions as meanings of words found in the dictionary. We are not used to thinking we have a choice in the definitions we accept and that those definitions can make a difference." The difference is that it's your success we're talking about so you should be the one setting the ground rules for its achievement.

Let's suppose that you subscribe to the more popular version of success that measures it in terms of titles, offices, and paychecks. Is there anything wrong with that? As a matter of fact, there is something wrong with that. It's not that there's anything inherently wrong with wanting or having these things; it's just that they're not true indicators of success. Many who have obtained these "trophies" have gotten little or no real satisfaction from them. I've personally known many people who, although they seemed to have it all, were, in fact, quite miserable. I've witnessed their nervous breakdowns, their ulcers, their heart attacks, and their divorces, and, yes, even their deaths, and I don't know about you, but dying is not in my definition of success.

By using these trophies as our measurement of success, we are setting ourselves up for failure—

- Some will work so hard to obtain these things that it literally will make them sick or kill them. They'll never be able to enjoy their success.
- Some will hardly work, but be given these things anyway, in spite of themselves. They'll never appreciate what they have or be satisfied by it.
- Some will become so obsessed with obtaining these things that they'll never have enough of it.
- Some will want these things, but never obtain them. They will become envious of, and resentful towards, those who have them, and disappointed with themselves. For them, there will be little or no hope.

A great many workers will fit into this last group. With success being unattainable for them they will see themselves as failures. Many will give up any hope of ever having a fancy title or a corner office or a big paycheck. To them, success will mean nothing more than not getting fired. How meaningful is that?

You deserve to be a success, not a failure. You must understand that having the fancy titles, the corner offices, and the big, fat paychecks is not what makes you a success, and that not having these things does not make you a failure. You can be a success, no matter what you do for a living, no matter how much money you make, and no matter what anybody else thinks. Nowhere is it written that you have to have a particular job, or make a specific amount of money, or have someone else's approval to be considered a success at work. That's for you to decide.

A good place to start

In deciding what success at work means to you, it might help you to have a basic premise on which to build your definition, so here goes:

Success at work means:

- Having a job
- Doing it well
- Getting satisfaction from it

It's a good premise because:

- It's attainable, which is good because it's better if you can celebrate your successes rather than be frustrated by your failures.
- It's meaningful, which is good because there's no point in attaining a goal that is not worth attaining.
- It will work for any type of job you might have. You can start using it right now.
- It has nothing to do with material rewards. You can be successful with or without the fancy titles, corner offices, and big paychecks.

- It allows you to know how it feels to be successful, which is good because once you feel it, you'll want more of it.
- It will lead to greater and greater rewards, including material rewards.

Read that last line again, and understand that the rewards will come, but you don't have to get obsessed about them or see them as being the be all and end all, the ultimate prize. All you have to do is focus on doing your job to the best of your ability. The ultimate prize will be the satisfaction you get from having done a good job. The rest is gravy.

Making your mark

Keeping in mind this premise that success is about having a job, doing it well, and getting satisfaction from it, now you need to make it personal by listing the good things you do at work that bring you satisfaction. Since "making your mark" means attaining success, let's call these success marks. Whenever you reach one of these marks, you need to celebrate. Now I'm not suggesting that you whip out a bottle of booze, jump up on a desk, and start shouting, "yeah me." That may be a bit much. A simple smile on your face or warm feeling in your heart will do, and an occasional treat wouldn't hurt either.

Success Marks
- When someone tells me I'm doing a good job.
- When I earn a bonus.
- When I do more today than I did yesterday.
- When I get a raise.
- When I'm given more responsibility.

- When someone thanks me.
- When I make someone smile.
- When customers ask for me by name.
- When I finish my work on time.
- When I help a co-worker.
- When I solve a problem.
- When I make a good decision.
- When I learn something new.
- When I help a customer.
- When I do the right thing.
- When I use my initiative to get something done.
- When I refuse to argue.
- When I admit that I made a mistake.
- When I take on a difficult task.
- When I serve my purpose (clean floors, good burgers...)

But are you ready and willing to succeed?

I have no doubt that you are more than capable of succeeding. Being able, however, is not enough. You must be ready and willing to succeed, ready and willing to do whatever it takes, even if that means:

- Questioning your values.
- Breaking old habits.
- Acquiring new skills.
- Making tough decisions.
- Taking unpopular stands.
- Separating from your friends.
- Being envied by some and resented by others.
- Working longer hours.
- Handling more responsibility.
- Being expected to do more.

I'm not suggesting that these things always happen, but sometimes they do, and you must be ready and willing to deal with them. Understand, however, that when you examine these things closer, you discover that they're not so bad after all—

- Everyone should question their values from time to time. Sometimes they're wrong and need to be changed.
- If you're replacing bad habits with good habits, that's a good thing.
- The more skills you have, the better.
- Most people will respect you for making tough decisions even when they disagree with them, and eventually, most people will forget they ever disagreed.
- It's the same as with tough decisions, and you're not in a popularity contest.
- This is where you find out who your true friends are.
- There will always be some folks who are happy for you and some who are not. With those who are envious, be humble; with those who are resentful, be understanding, but be careful too.
- The longer you work, the more you get done and the more you earn. What's the problem with that?
- With more responsibilities comes greater privileges and greater satisfaction.
- The more you do, the more valuable you will become.

So, are you ready, willing, and able to succeed at work? I think you are. I certainly hope you are, because in my mind, and hopefully in yours, FAILURE IS NOT AN OPTION.

SUMMARY

- How you define success will help to determine whether or not you achieve it.
- True success is measured not by the material rewards you get for it, but by the satisfaction you get from it.
- Success at work means having a job, doing it well, and getting satisfaction from it.
- Failure is not an option (unless you decide to make it one.)

Assignments:

1. Make a list of your success marks. Read it every day before you go to work.
2. Think of ways you can celebrate when you make your marks, and try not to get fired or arrested for doing them.

Lesson Four: Having the Ability to Succeed

Objectives:

1. To appreciate the abilities you have, and make use of them.
2. To learn some of the skills you can use to be successful.
3. To learn how and why you should better yourself physically, mentally, emotionally, and spiritually.

He is able who thinks he is able.—Buddha

You have the ability to succeed. You don't have to have an IQ of 200, a photographic memory, a body to die for, or a father who owns an NFL franchise, and it makes no difference whether you're young or old, male or female, a college graduate or a high school dropout, or whether you're black, white, brown, yellow, or green. I take that last part back—I can see some issues with you being green, unless, of course, you happen to be Kermit the Frog or the Incredible Hulk.

You are as capable as the next person, and for a very good reason—you, and everyone else, have a God given ability to control your own thoughts, actions, and emotions, and in so doing, succeed. You have the ability, but the question is will you exercise the control? As

I see it, there are only three things that can prevent you from succeeding:

- Not believing in your abilities
- Not using your abilities
- Not breathing

Do you know what a self fulfilling prophecy is? Well it works like this—you believe that something's going to happen, so you act as though it will happen; and because you act as though it will happen, it happens. It happens because you make it happen. And that is why so many fail. Believing they will fail anyway, they make little or no attempt to succeed, and because they make no attempt, they inevitably fail.

Far too many workers do not believe in their own abilities, and as a consequence, fail to use the abilities they have. They spend way too much time feeling sorry for themselves, and not enough time doing their jobs. They will work hard, however, at tearing down workers who do succeed with comments such as, "he probably stepped on a lot of people to get where he is," "she must have slept her way to the top," "he must have known someone to get that job," and "she probably got that job because she's a woman."

How come they're not successful? If you were to ask them, they'd probably claim to be "victims of circumstances," being disadvantaged by a boss who hates them or some jealous co-workers or some handicap or prejudice. Now I'm not so naïve not to know that some people do face bigger obstacles, but I also know that many folks who have faced such obstacles, have overcome them. (See lesson seventeen for more on overcoming obstacles.)

What I'm trying to say is that you have incredible abilities, some of which you may not even be aware of. You should feel good about your abilities, and good about yourself. It helps when you do, because as Spencer Johnson and Ken Blanchard wrote, "People who feel good about themselves produce good results." And feeling good about yourself also shields you from those who would tear you down. They can't tear you down if you don't let them. In the words of Eleanor Roosevelt, "No one can make you feel inferior without your consent."

As good as you are

So now we both know that you're an incredible person. Congratulations! You have this ability to control what you think, what you do, and how you feel. With this ability, not only can you change yourself, but you can influence others to change too. This is no small feat, and you should appreciate its significance.

Having the ability and using it, however, are two different things. All of us have the ability; few of us use it. Few of us exercise any control over our thoughts, actions, and emotions. We think without acting, act without thinking, let emotions guide our actions, and let others tell us what we should believe, how we should act, and how we should feel.

We hesitate to use our abilities because we fear criticism, failure, and yes, even success. We succumb to stress, illness, idleness, and fatigue, all of which sap our abilities to the point of rendering us unable to use them.

You can't let this happen to you. If you don't use your abilities, they will be useless to you, and no better than having no abilities at all. You must protect yourself from the forces that will sap your abilities, and at the same time, work to improve on the abilities you have. You can never let your guard down, never become complacent, never stop learning, and never stop growing. There is always more to learn and always room to grow. As good as you are, you can always get better.

Getting better

Believing in yourself and in your abilities is the obvious first step in getting better, but it's not the only step you can take. You can also:

- Find something you can get excited about.
- Learn new skills and sharpen the skills you have.
- Get yourself in shape—physically, mentally, emotionally, and spiritually.

Finding something to get excited about—History has taught us repeatedly that people and organizations having a strong purpose or mission to accomplish will achieve great things. Those who worked in our country's space program had a mission, and they conquered the stars. You don't have to aim for the stars, but you can find yourself a purpose, something you can get excited about. Maybe it could be:

- Giving your best effort.
- Learning new things.
- Helping those in need.
- Setting a good example for others.
- Being a good parent.
- Achieving financial independence.
- Having a job, doing it well, and getting satisfaction from it.

Keeping your mind focused on your purpose will guide you to making decisions and taking actions that will move you closer to achieving your purpose and protect you from the things that will move you farther away from it.

Sharpening the skills you have and acquiring new skills—There's an old Chinese proverb which says, "To do his work well, a workman must first sharpen his skills." With the demands of the workplace today being what they are, you must not only sharpen the skills you have, but acquire new skills as well. Here, we're not talking about the soft skills taught in Working 101, but the hard, technical skills that are required for specific jobs.

If, for example, you were a nurse's aide working in a hospital or nursing home, you would have to know how to take vital signs, assist with patient transfers, and make beds. Those would be some of the technical requirements of your job. Those you will have to learn at work, but keep in mind as you're learning that it's your job you are learning to do, and that if you don't learn to do it well, it might become someone else's job. So pay attention when you have an opportunity to learn. If your company offers training, go because you want to, not because you have to.

Many technical skills are very job specific, but there are some that could be of benefit to you no matter what type of job you have. You don't have to have these skills, but as my mother used to remind me, it wouldn't hurt to have them.

<u>Wouldn't Hurt Skills</u>

1. A second language. The non-English speaking population is growing in this country, as is

the influence of Japanese and European businesses and investors.

2. Computer literacy. Computers are everywhere, and while you don't have to be a computer whiz, it helps if you understand what the whiz kids are talking about.

3. Typing. Handwritten or badly typed memos are not held in high regard.

4. Speed reading. Information is both important and abundant. The ability to read faster and comprehend better will serve you well.

5. Shorthand. For the same reason that you'd want to read faster, you'd also want to take notes faster.

6. Memorization. If you're like most people, you remember only a small portion of everything you see or hear. It would help if you could remember more. Now, where was I? Oh yes,

7. Vocabulary. A large vocabulary, according to Denis Waitley, "characterizes the more successful persons, regardless of their occupations." Most people know enough words to get by, but not enough to get ahead.

8. Public speaking. There may come a time when you'll need to speak in front of a group. If you're not prepared to do that, your time will pass before you know it.

9. Writing. You may have to fill out an application, send a memo, or do a report. If you don't understand the fine points of spelling, grammar, and style, you will expose your limitations for all to see.

10. Supervision. Many workers who are promoted to supervisory positions are ill equipped to be good supervisors, and so, they fail.

DID YOU KNOW? According to the U.S. Department of Labor, the top skills in demand today, listed in no particular order, are:

- Problem solving
- Vocational & technical
- Human relations
- Computer programming
- Teaching & training
- Science & math
- Money management
- Foreign language
- Business management

Getting in shape—The importance of getting yourself in shape, as it relates to your success and happiness at work, is indisputable. You can't do your best if you're not at your best, physically, mentally, emotionally, and spiritually. Although this is not a book about physical fitness, stress management, emotional stability, and spirituality, and I am no expert in any of them, their importance and relevance to your performance at work is too important to be overlooked.

Becoming physically fit—Physically fit workers are more productive workers—

- They miss fewer days due to illness or injury, which is important because you can't do a good job if you're not there to do it!
- They have more energy, strength, enthusiasm, and confidence.
- They are less prone to accidents, less likely to crack under pressure, and less likely to make mistakes.

- They get more respect from their co-workers and customers because, as research has shown, people respond better to other people who are taller, thinner, more confident, better dressed, and better looking. Studies have shown that overweight workers earn less on average than their co-workers. They are perceived by many to have a lesser work ethic, and whether or not this is true doesn't matter as long as people believe that it is.

These sound like good reasons to get yourself into shape physically. I can offer you some advice on how to go about doing that, but I suggest that you seek more advice elsewhere. It would make sense that if you want to know how to be thin, a good place to start would be to talk to a thin person.

- Eat right. My best advice is not to go on any diets. For me, any word with "die" in it should be hazardous to your health.
- Exercise regularly. There's almost as many workout routines and exercise equipment as there are diets, and you know how many diets there are. The routines will only work if you follow them and the equipment will only help if you use it, so my advice is to find something you like doing so you'll keep doing it.
- Get some rest and relaxation. Relax with a good book, a hot bath, your favorite music, time with your kids, time away from your kids, a nice dinner out, a glass of wine, two glasses of wine, or a massage. Get a good night's sleep, and on occasion, take a nice nap. It will energize your body and

protect it from the normal wear and tear it takes. But for goodness sake, don't do these things while you're at work or you might get a memo:

Memo to All Employees

Please do not fall asleep on the job. This makes it very difficult for management to distinguish between workers who appear to be dead and those who actually are dead. This creates serious delays in the removal of dead bodies and in the completion of workers compensation reports. We can no longer wait until quitting time when those of you who appear to be dead come miraculously back to life. Thank you for your consideration. Management.

- Practice good safety habits. Even though the workplace is safer today than it ever was, it is still not as safe as it could be. If you get hurt, you're not going to be very productive.

DID YOU KNOW? Every year, there are 2,000,000 on the job injuries, of which, 100,000 lead to permanent damage, and 10,000 to 15,000 lead to death. Every year, 500,000,000 workdays are lost due to illness and injury.

- Don't smoke. Smokers are absent two and a half times more than non-smokers, and they spend more time on breaks.
- Don't use drugs, and drink only in moderation, if at all. By all means, don't come to work under the influence or use on the job.

DID YOU KNOW? According to the U.S. Department of Labor, 20% of workers claimed they had to work harder, redo work, cover for a co-worker, or be put in harm's way because of co-workers with drug or alcohol problems.

DID YOU KNOW? According to the Department of Labor, alcohol and drug problems were directly responsible for 35% of all absences, 47% of all accidents, and 40% of all job related fatalities.

- Listen to your body. Pain, fatigue, itching, sweating, shaking, fever, and chills are only some of the ways that your body tells you when it's time to stop doing whatever it is you're doing to it. Your body can only take so much abuse. Sometimes, you just have to back off, take a break, and maybe get some help. If you're sick, you're sick. Stay home and get better so you can get back to work as soon as possible. Don't try to be a hero. All you're going to do at work is make yourself even sicker and make everyone else sick too. On the other hand, don't stay home if you're not sick. Do your job to the best of your ability, but listen to your body when it's telling you to slow down or stop. Never work so long and so hard that you become too sick, too tired, or too dead to enjoy the fruits of your labor. Your job is a big part of who you are, but you are so much more than just your job.

DID YOU KNOW? A study by CCH, Inc. revealed that an estimated 62% of call-ins are for reasons having nothing to do with actual illness. An online article spoke of one genius who, in the true tradition of "my dog ate my homework," used "my cat unplugged my alarm clock" as his excuse for not coming in.

DID YOU KNOW? A Kronos Workforce Institute study of 1188 workers found that 89% had called in sick to attend or to watch a sporting event.

- Get help when you need it. If you're having problems with your health, with drugs or alcohol, with your marriage or your kids, or with your finances, consider swallowing your pride and asking for help. Why? Because sooner or later, your personal problems will lead to performance problems on the job. Talk to your boss about your problem before he has to talk to you about your performance. He might understand; he might offer help. It's worth a try. FYI, your boss, along with everyone else at work probably already knows about your problem. If you've told even one person, everyone knows.
- Practice good grooming and hygiene, and do it before you come to work. If they wanted you to fix your hair or apply your make-up at work, they would have installed mirrors on your desk!

Memo to All Employees
If it is necessary for us kiss your butt to get you to do anything around here, please have the decency to wash it first before you come to work. Thank you for your consideration. Management.

- Dress for success. Follow the three C's of dressing for work—Clean, Comfortable, and

Conservative. Don't wear clothes that are dirty, wrinkled, too tight, too loose, too revealing, or otherwise too distracting. People should be talking about what you're doing, not what you're wearing. An old friend of mine used to say, "I may not know what I'm doing, but I sure look good doing it." She looked good on the unemployment line too.

Becoming mentally fit—What I should say is staying mentally fit. A 1992 United Nations report characterized job stress as the "20th Century Disease." By all indications, the 21st century will be no different. Job stress is a reality we all have to deal with. As Malcolm Forbes suggested, "If you have a job with no aggravations, you don't have a job."

DID YOU KNOW? In a Gallup Poll taken in 2000, 80% of workers said they felt stressed by their jobs. 50% of those workers felt they needed help in dealing with it. Anger, violence, threats, and intimidation were all identified as symptoms of job stress.

DID YOU KNOW? In an Integra survey done in 2000, 19% of workers said they had to quit their jobs because of stress.

What can stress do to you? What can't it do? It can render you incapable of controlling your thoughts, actions, and emotions. It can cause headaches, rashes, ulcers, hair loss, weight loss, weight gain, nervous breakdowns, and heart attacks. It can cause people to drink or do drugs, and it can even kill you. An estimated 75% of all visits to the doctors' office are directly or indirectly related to stress as are, I imagine, a great many visits to the cemetery.

At home, stress can break up your marriage, destroy your friendships, and alienate you from your children. At work, it can break your concentration, destroy your motivation, cause you to make mistakes, make you susceptible to illness and injury, ruin your credibility, or get you fired.

What causes stress at work? In his book, The Stress Check, Cary C. Cooper provides a list of those things he believes cause stress at work—

- Too much work (overload)
- Too little work (boredom)
- Deadlines and time pressures
- Physical and mental fatigue
- Travel
- Long hours
- Change
- Repercussions from mistakes
- Excessive phone calls, e-mails, and meetings
- Unrealistic expectations from supervisors
- Rude customers
- Lazy co-workers
- Role ambiguity ("What am I supposed to do?")
- Role conflict ("Why must I do this?")
- Responsibility for others
- Job insecurity
- Lack of information (being kept "in the dark")
- Lack of opportunity
- Lack of appreciation

DID YOU KNOW? In a poll conducted in 2000, 50% of workers said they were clearly worried about losing their jobs.

There are two important things you must know about this list—one, the biggest cause of your stress at work is not on the list, and two, if not for the biggest cause, most of the things on the list would not be on it. As it turns out, the biggest cause of your stress at work is none other than YOU.

When you waste time, and have to play catch-up to get your work done, you make more mistakes, miss more deadlines, and put added pressure on yourself, leaving your boss with little to appreciate.

When, instead of focusing on the task at hand, you focus on what everybody else is doing, your job doesn't get done, expectations go unmet, and longer hours are needed to get things back on track. Losing track of what you should be doing, role ambiguity sets in as you wonder, "What was I supposed to be doing?"

When you act on information that you haven't verified, you say and do things that are hurtful to others and embarrassing to you. If you're being "kept in the dark," it's because you "turned out the lights." When you take on responsibilities that you're not prepared to handle, you get overloaded, pressured, and overwhelmed by the long hours, the changes, and the responsibility of having to answer for the actions of other people.

You are, indeed, the biggest cause of your own stress. That's the bad news. The good news is that you are the biggest cause of your own stress. Yes, you read that correctly. It's bad because you're hurting yourself; it's good because if you're the one doing this to yourself, you can just as easily undo what you have done. You can start by not putting yourself into stressful situations, and learning the basic, soft skills will help you with that. You can learn how to handle stress, but for that, you must hear the other side of the story.

Our story began by examining the causes of stress at work. The other side of the story is about the stress that is caused. Have you ever noticed that two people, under the same stressful circumstances, can have completely different reactions, how one can feel stress, and the other not, how one can completely fall apart, and the other rise to the occasion?

This is of great significance, because it teaches us that the things that can cause us stress do not always cause us stress, that when we feel stressed, it is not so much from what causes it, but from how we react to it. What happens to us is never as important as how we react to what happens.

Sometimes we can avoid the things that cause us stress, and sometimes we can't; sometimes we can control these things, and sometimes we can't; but always we can control how we react to these things. The plain and simple truth is that nothing can cause us to feel stressed unless we allow it to do so.

Is your boss breathing down your neck? Are your co-workers dumping all the work on you? Is some customer being a jerk? Did someone forget to clean the coffee pot? So what? Why must you make yourself sick over every little thing? I mean, in the bigger scheme of things, how important is this stuff? Is anyone even going to remember these things in a day or two? Probably not.

It's not the big things that bother us so much. When something terrible happens, like a death in the family, we deal with it by mourning, remembering, and moving on, all with the support of our families and friends. But with these annoying little things that happen to us, there is no support. These little things sneak up on us, and accumulate, and eventually, we snap, we crackle, and we pop.

Mike Jacobs

That doesn't have to happen. If you keep these strategies in mind, it won't happen:

1. Learn the skills that will stop you from putting yourself into stressful situations.
2. Try to avoid the people and things you know will bother you.
3. If you can't avoid them, learn how to deal with them—walk away, count to ten (or a hundred if you must), learn to compromise...If someone says or does something mean, selfish, or stupid, laugh it off and remind yourself that it's their problem, not yours. It is their problem.
4. If you can't handle it, and it gets to you, find ways to relieve the stress such as exercise, relaxation, or prayer.
5. If all else fails, learn to live with it. Eventually, you can get used to just about anything.

Becoming emotionally fit—There's nothing wrong with being emotional, as long as you control your emotions and not let your emotions control you.

There should be, as we know, a connection between thought and action. When the connection is not there, bad things happen. Thoughts not acted upon accomplish nothing; actions taken without thought accomplish things that would be better not accomplished. Many good people have regretted not saying what they thought about saying and not doing what they thought about doing. Many more have "put their foot in their mouth," or "stuck their nose where it didn't belong," or found themselves "up the creek without a paddle," all because they forgot to think before they acted.

When you add emotions to the mix, the waters get even muddier. With emotions, your thoughts grow stronger and your actions grow bolder. That's good if your emotions are positive, but bad if they're not. Negative emotions can drive people to do the worst of things.

In *Think and Grow Rich*, Napoleon Hill suggested that there are seven major positive emotions—desire, faith, love, sex, enthusiasm, romance, and hope, and seven major negative emotions—fear, jealousy, hatred, revenge, greed, superstition, and anger. He strongly recommended that you draw as much as possible from the positives and avoid as, much as possible, the negatives.

I want you to think about this. Think about how desire and enthusiasm can improve your chances of succeeding, and of how anger and jealousy can improve your chances of failing. The positives build you up; the negatives tear you down. It's for you to decide in which direction you wish to be heading.

Nobody, including me, can tell you how to feel. That's for you to decide. They're your emotions. All I can say is, know when you're being "emotional," and think carefully before you act on your emotions.

Becoming spiritually fit—Don't worry. I'm not going to preach. As far as I'm concerned, it's "to each his own." I just want you to know that I, personally, have had many ups and downs in my fifty one years on the job, and that I owe a great deal of my success, and the better part of my ability to survive hard times, to my unwavering and absolute faith in God.

I truly believe that The Lord gave us this incredible power to control our own thoughts, actions, and emotions, not just to have it, but to use it for our own well being and for the greater good of all. Not to believe in ourselves and not to use our abilities is, to me, downright sinful.

Others have strongly recommended the need to find one's spiritual self as a prerequisite to success on the job. Napoleon Hill and Deepak Chopra are two of the better known advocates of this idea. At the very least, it's something to consider.

SUMMARY

- You have the ability to control your own thoughts, actions, and emotions, and with that comes the ability to succeed.
- You are a very capable person, but as good as you are, you can always get better.
- When you find something to get excited about, celebrate every time you do it.
- Your skills must always be sharpened and new ones should always be sought.
- Healthy workers are more productive workers.
- It's okay to be emotional as long as you know that you are, and understand its potential effect on your actions.

Assignments:

1. At work tomorrow, every time someone or something upsets you, do the following: stop what you're doing and say to yourself, "Why am I getting upset? Is this really worth getting sick over?

Lesson Five:
Taking Responsibility for Your Success

Objectives:

1. To understand the importance of the choices you make.
2. To learn how to make good choices.
3. To learn how to make your own decisions and solve your own problems.
4. To accept responsibility for your success.

To work is both a privilege and a responsibility. To enjoy the privilege, you must accept the responsibility. If you are to succeed, you must accept responsibility for that success. Why? Because you are responsible for everything that happens to you.

"How can I be responsible for everything that happens to me at work? My boss tells me what to do; my customers tell me what they want; and my co-workers do whatever they want to do. My boss makes all the decisions, and when I have a problem, I take it to him. So what the heck are you talking about?" There you go with your questions again.

I'll explain—you are responsible for most of what happens to you; you will be held responsible for much of the rest of what happens; and, you will always be responsible for how you react to what happens, regardless of who is responsible for making it happen in the first place. As we learned in lesson four, how you react to what happens is more important than what happens.

Forget about what everybody else is doing. They're going to do what they're going to do, and when it's done, it's done. Focus your attention on what you're doing. That's the only place you have any real control anyway.

Now that we have that out of the way, let's talk about what it really means to accept responsibility. I believe it means:

- Deciding what success means to you. (as we discussed in lesson three).
- Deciding where you want to go and how you want to get there. Setting goals and making plans to attain those goals. (setting a course)
- Taking the initiative. (getting on course)
- Making good choices. (staying on course)
- Making no excuses. (getting back on course)
- Admitting your mistakes. (getting back on course again)
- Making your own decisions.
- Solving your own problems.

Setting goals/making plans

Begin with the end in mind.—Stephen Covey

Either you know what you want, or you don't. When you know what you want, you're more likely to get it; when you don't know what you want, you'll get what you get, whether you want it or not, whether you like it or not, and whether it's good for you or not.

Everyone should set goals at work; not everyone does. A great many workers honestly believe that setting goals, just like making decisions, is something only managers do. More than a few have been heard to say, "I just do what I'm told."

That's a shame, because managers are not the only ones who should be setting goals or making decisions. As a matter of fact, businesses run better when employees are helping to establish goals and making day to day decisions, leaving managers free to set broader objectives and make bigger decisions.

There are any number of goals you can set for yourself at work, including:

- To be the best at what you do.
- To earn more money.
- To get a promotion.
- To learn new skills.
- To get more experience.
- To be more productive.
- To serve more customers.
- To get fewer complaints.
- To get done on time.
- To make fewer mistakes.
- To waste less time.
- To get a better performance evaluation.
- To be more helpful to co-workers.
- To come to work on time.
- To find new and better ways to do things.
- To make better choices.

I'm sure you can think of more. A good one I like to recommend is known in some circles as the Plus One strategy, but I like to refer to it as the "do one more than you did before" approach. It's really simple—for whatever you do, i.e. make sales calls, enter data, handle complaints, etc. you aim to do one more than you did before, i.e. the day before, the month before, the year before, etc. It's a good way to challenge yourself. Now, keep in mind that you're not going to do more every time you try, but you will most certainly get more done if you keep on trying.

Whatever goals you set, try to make them specific and measurable so you'll know when you reach them, challenging yet attainable, worthy of your time and efforts, and consistent with your purpose and the company's objectives.

Taking the initiative

DID YOU KNOW? In a recent online poll of 7,760 workers, 55% listed initiative as the most important factor in getting ahead at work. In comparison, nothing else got more than 17%.

While most workers generally recognize the importance of initiative in getting ahead at work, few actually use their initiative to do so. Why is this?

- They don't want to get stuck doing someone else's work.
- They're afraid to make any mistakes.
- They don't want their boss to get mad at them.
- They don't want anyone to think they're "kissing up" to the boss.
- They don't want to appear as being overly ambitious.
- They don't want to do anything that's not in their job description.

- They don't want to "rock the boat."
- They're afraid to be criticized.
- They're not comfortable doing new things.

And on and on and on…What they fail to realize is that by not using their initiative, they are missing out on some real opportunities to get ahead. You see, experience has taught us that being the first to do anything is always worth something. Sure, you can wait, but it may be too late. As Abraham Lincoln once said, "Things may come to those who wait, but only the things left by those who hustle."

I can promise you that you won't get into any trouble using your initiative, provided you:

1. Think about what you're going to do before you do it.
2. Keep your boss informed of what you're doing and how it's going.
3. Ask for help if you need it.
4. Work within company policies and procedures unless you get permission to do otherwise.
5. Do something that benefits the company.

If whatever you're doing doesn't work, don't sweat it. At least your boss will know that you tried, and that means a lot.

It's easier to ask for forgiveness than it is to ask for permission.—Old Jesuit principle

Making good choices

There is always a choice about the way you do your work, even if there is not a choice about the work itself.—Stephen Lundin

Mike Jacobs

You are who you are, what you are, and where you are because of the choices you have made. You choose what to believe; you choose what to do. You make choices every day, all day long.

- You choose to either come to work or stay home.
- You choose to either work hard or hardly work.
- You choose to either be positive or negative.
- You choose to either accept responsibility or place blame elsewhere.
- You choose to either serve others first or serve only yourself.
- You choose to either spend your time being productive or waste it.
- You choose to either check information out or accept it blindly.
- You choose to either embrace change or resist it.
- You choose to either face up to your challenges or run from them.
- You choose to either forgive and forget or carry grudges and never forget.
- You choose to either make plans or make excuses.

You make choices all the time, even though you may not always be aware that you're making them. Perhaps it's time you became aware.

Be aware that when you're being rude to a customer, you're choosing to be rude; when you're late to work every day, you're choosing to be late; when you're wasting time at work, you're choosing to waste time; when you're missing deadlines, you're choosing to miss them; and when you're ignoring instructions, you're choosing to ignore them.

It's the workers who make these poor choices who are the very same workers who are dissatisfied, disgruntled, and disinterested, and no, it is not a coincidence. The absolute truth is that the real difference between workers who are successful and workers who are not, has nothing to do with their education, their experience, their intelligence, their skin color, their age, their sex, or their sexual preference; it has everything to do with the choices they make. Workers who are happy and successful make better choices than workers who are not so successful.

The significance of the previous paragraph cannot be overstated. If I were you, I'd read it again. I think it should give hope to all workers, no matter who they are, what they look like, or what they do for a living. It tells us that anyone who wants to be happy and successful at work can be happy and successful by choosing to think and act as happy and successful workers do. *Working 101* will show you how to do that.

We choose the paths we travel on, and unfortunately, many of us choose the wrong path. The road to success is the road less traveled, hence the growing job dissatisfaction we are seeing. So why is this the case?

There appear to be seven main reasons for the inability or the reluctance of workers to make the kinds of choices that would clearly benefit them—low self esteem, the fear of failure or criticism, the fear of success, the resistance to change, laziness, the fear of confrontation, and the lack of information.

Low self esteem

Too many of those who begin at the bottom never manage to lift their heads high enough to be seen by opportunity, so they remain at the bottom. It should be remembered, also, that the outlook from the bottom is not so very bright or encouraging. It has a tendency to kill off ambition.—Napoleon Hill

Many workers truly believe that they are not deserving of success, and that even if they tried to succeed, they would not succeed because they don't deserve to. So, as a result of this self fulfilling prophecy, they fail to succeed. What a surprise!

The choices they make, of course, are not the choices they should be making. After all, why should they choose to think and act as successful people think and act when they don't deserve to be successful anyway?

The fear of failure or criticism

People who are afraid to fail will make little or no effort to succeed. How ironic it is that their failure will be a result of their fear of failure!

Closely related to this fear is the fear of criticism. Nobody really likes to be criticized, but some folks are so afraid of it that they will go out of their way to avoid it. They won't do anything that could possibly draw criticism to them. They choose not to do things to avoid making mistakes, and they choose not to admit to the mistakes they make.

The fear of success

Believe it or not, the fear of success is just as destructive to some people as the fear of failure. Success, to these folks, means hard work, added pressures, greater responsibilities, longer hours, etc. They choose to avoid these things.

The resistance to change

Some people will resist change even when they sense that the change will do them good. They do what they do because it's the way they've always done it. Yes, they're in a rut, but it's their rut, and as far as they're concerned, it's fine just the way it is.

Laziness

Many avoid the road to success because it appears to be a difficult road to take. Instead, they choose to take the path of least resistance. Rather than do what they know should be done, they do only what they're told; rather than take the time to do things right, they look for shortcuts to get it done quickly; and rather than do as much as they can do, they do only what they have to and as little as they can, as long as they can get away with it. To them, success looks like hard work, and, in a sense, they're right—it is much easier to fail than it is to succeed.

The fear of confrontation

Many avoid, if they can, confrontation. They choose not to make others mad. They may want to do the right thing, but will do, instead, what everyone else is doing, or what they think others want them to do, or what others believe to be the "politically correct" thing to do. They choose, by default, to let others choose for them.

Mike Jacobs

The lack of information

Most workers who make the wrong choices make them because nobody ever showed them how to make the right choices. As we said earlier, there is a serious lack of good information available to workers.

I must tell you that none of these things that we've just talked about can cause you to make the wrong choices unless you choose to let them. The lack of information is easily overcome by seeking out the information you need. *Working 101* is a great place to begin your search. The fear of failure, criticism, success, or confrontation is nothing more than a state of mind, and as long as you haven't yet lost your mind, you can always change its state. Laziness is nothing but an excuse, and excuses are nothing but lies you tell yourself. This can be overcome by accepting the truth. And the resistance to change is nothing more than a fear of the unknown and a matter of habit. Fear of the unknown can be overcome by getting information, and bad habits can be changed too. The unwillingness to change is a decision you make and the inability to change is only a perception. Decisions and perceptions both can be changed.

NEWSFLASH!!! In the entire history of mankind, very little if anything has ever been accomplished immediately after someone said, "Because that's the way we've always done it."

Making no excuses

You're there to work, not to get out of working. So stop making excuses and placing the blame on everyone but yourself. It's not your boss, your co-workers, your customers, your spouse, your kids, your parents, your cat, your teachers, the President, the communists, the FBI, the CIA, the economy, or some aliens from another planet who made your choices for you, you made them yourself.

If you have some kind of problem, if you're not as happy or as successful as you'd like to be, don't waste your time trying to find someone you can blame it on. They're not going to admit anything anyway, and they're just going to get angry and defensive. Angry and defensive people are of little or no help to you.

Instead of trying to find fault with others, try to find solutions to your problems. When you do that, people will be more willing to help. Look, also, at yourself. Ask yourself, "Did I do something to make this happen? Could I have done anything differently? What can I do now to make this better?" If you must point fingers, be sure you're standing in front of a mirror.

See excuses for what they really are—lies you tell yourself and others, lies, that if told enough times, you will come to believe. You will come to believe them, but few others will. Most people can usually see right through them.

Having said that, I happen to know that a great many people make excuses all the time in an attempt to get out of doing their work. God forbid they should have to put in eight hours in a day and have to work too. That would be asking too much. So, in honor of these fine folks, I present for your reading pleasure, (and not for your use) the most common excuses used:

Top Ten Classic Work Excuses

1. That's not my job. (my table, my station, my department, my customer...)

2. It's not in my job description. (my scope of practice, my area of responsibility, my budget, my contract, my agreement…)
3. Nobody ever told me how to do it. (what to do) (Note: This is often preceded by "I'm new here," which some workers apparently say for months or even years.)
4. There isn't enough time.
5. They don't pay me enough to do that.
6. Nobody else is doing it, so why should I?
7. Nobody appreciates what I do, so why bother?
8. If I do too much, my co-workers will resent me.
9. If I do more than what's expected, they'll keep expecting more from me.
10. I'll never get ahead because I'm a woman. (Black, Hispanic, Asian, Jewish, Catholic, gay, disabled, uneducated, too old, too young, too fat, too skinny, too short, too tall…)

You'll never get ahead if you keep spouting this garbage all day, and I'll give you my top ten reasons why:

1. It is your job to help all customers or to get someone else to help.
2. Nowhere in your job description does it say you can't do anything else.
3. You could always ask what to do (or use your initiative!)
4. There will be enough time if you use it wisely.
5. If you're cashing those paychecks, you are being paid enough to do it.
6. What your co-workers are doing has nothing to do with what you should be doing.

7. You're in this for satisfaction, not appreciation. (P.S. just because no one shows you appreciation, it doesn't mean they don't appreciate you.)
8. Your success has nothing to do with what your co-workers think.
9. When they start expecting more from you, that's when you can start expecting those raises and promotions.
10. If you're facing discrimination for who you are, the best way to overcome it is by what you do. (Doing your job poorly will not help to overcome discrimination.)

Admitting your mistakes

Nobody's perfect, but, then, you don't have to be. Anyone who has a job, and tries to do it, will make some mistakes. Bosses know this, and expect this. They know that the only workers who never make mistakes are the ones who have never done anything and never tried. You won't find such workers on the Forbes list of the richest people in America, nor will you find them on too many payrolls. People like that don't stay employed for long.

Why do people make mistakes? Believe it or not, it's not because they're stupid, although sometimes, you do have to wonder. They make mistakes because they are:

- In a hurry.
- Under pressure.
- Sick.
- Tired.
- Sick and tired.

Mike Jacobs

- Misinformed.
- Disinterested.
- Overloaded.
- Under the influence.
- Not thinking.
- Trying too hard.
- Doing work they're not trained for or suited to.
- Not paying attention.
- Human.

They're not paying attention because of all the distractions around them—loud and annoying noises, poor lighting, extreme temperatures, meddling co-workers, rude customers, people they can't take their eyes off of, problems at home they can't stop thinking about, plans for the weekend they won't stop talking about, breaking stories in the news that no one can stop talking about...

It's easy to make mistakes when you've lost your focus on the task at hand. Most mistakes can be avoided if you are aware of the people and the things that are distracting you, and you remove the distractions or put off the task at hand until the distractions remove themselves.

It is okay to make mistakes, but you need to admit when you make them. Many workers won't do that, but will, instead, cover them up or blame them on somebody else. Usually, they do this for one or more of these three reasons—laziness, pride, and fear.

People do get lazy from time to time. Admitting their mistakes will mean they'll have to do whatever they did all over again. They figure that if they ignore the mistake long enough, either no one else will notice it or someone else will fix it. That's what you call "wishful thinking."

Some people are too proud to admit they made a mistake. They want to maintain a perception of perfection. In reality, it's more of a deception than a perception. They're deceiving others and themselves, and destroying any chance they could have had to learn from their mistakes.

By far, the most common reason for not admitting mistakes is fear. Most people are afraid of being criticized or punished. They're in no hurry to get called into the boss's office to get chewed out.

Yes, despite all the books and seminars on how to be a better boss, there are still quite a few bosses around who help to foster this fear by going out of their way to scare their workers, by looking for opportunities to catch their workers making mistakes, so they can dish out some discipline. And for what? So they can let everyone know who's in charge? These bosses subscribe to what is affectionately known as the "heads will roll" philosophy of management.

Well, workers, naturally, are not too fond of this philosophy:

Memo to Management

We, the employees of this company, would like to inform you of our objection to the new "heads will roll" policy. We like our heads just where they are right now. Therefore, effective immediately, we will no longer admit when we make mistakes. We understand that this will create serious difficulties for the company, but these measures are necessary. We respect the fact that you have the right to set policies, but we question where your heads were at when you set this one. The Employees.

To avoid making mistakes, workers will do less work, and will admit to the mistakes they make less often.

61

It all becomes some kind of game, with bosses playing "gotcha," and workers playing "catch me if you can." It's a game nobody wins, and it will never end until bosses realize that it's better to be respected than to be feared, and workers realize that it's better to be honest than to get caught in a lie. Both workers and their bosses must realize, too, that mistakes are never as important as the manner in which they are handled.

This is not a game we're all playing. If we are to be effective at running a business, people must be judged, not by the mistakes they make, but by the way they handle those mistakes. Unfortunately, although everyone makes mistakes, not everyone knows how to handle the mistakes they make.

How to handle mistakes

- Check your work to see if you made any mistakes.
- Correct the mistakes if you can.
- If you can't correct them, or if any damage has been done, admit that you made them.
- With or without help, get them corrected before things get worse.
- Learn what you can from them.
- Be careful not to repeat them.

The obvious first step is to look for mistakes, to be critical of your work before someone else has to criticize you for it. Then, of course, if it's something easily fixed, fix it. Don't move on to another project before you finish the one you're on now. Otherwise, you'll forget.

If you can't fix it, or even if you can, but the damage has already been done, own up to it. Tell your boss what happened. I guarantee that you'll be much better off if you tell your boss, "I made a mistake, but I fixed it," than if your boss has to tell you, "You made a mistake, and you better fix it."

When you own up to your mistakes, good things will start to happen, and that's because you will earn the respect of your boss and your co-workers for having the courage and good sense to admit your mistakes, and when they have more respect for you, they'll be more willing to help you.

Mistakes should be corrected because left alone, they're not going to miraculously correct themselves. If you haven't corrected them, you need to get it done, with or without help. And by the way, there's nothing wrong with asking for help. There is, however, something very wrong with not correcting a mistake solely because you're too stubborn or nervous to ask for help.

A man who knows he has committed a mistake and doesn't correct it is committing another mistake.-Confucius

From your mistakes, and from your efforts to correct them, there's a lot you can learn. At the very least, you can learn what you shouldn't be doing, and that's a good thing to learn.

By learning from your mistakes, you become a better worker, and you improve your chances of not making the same mistake again. This is important because although your boss will probably be patient with, and forgiving of, your mistakes, his patience and forgiveness will eventually wear thin. Besides, why make the same mistake over and over when there are so many more mistakes you can be making?

Making your own decisions

If you want to make better choices, you should have some idea of how to go about doing that. Making choices, or decisions, should not be that hard to do, but for many workers, it is hard. I'm going to try, however, to make it a little easier for you.

Decision making is something you must learn, no matter what your job is. More and more decisions being made today are being made by non-supervisory employees. It's a trend that will, in all likelihood, continue because it makes a lot of sense. The people who are most affected by a decision should be the people who are making those decisions.

There's another very good reason for you to be learning how to make better decisions—if you always depend on others to decide for you, you will always have to depend on them, and you will never develop the ability or the courage to decide for yourself.

So if you're going to make decisions, here are some things you should keep in mind:

- It doesn't matter how many decisions you make, but how well you make your decisions. The best workers and managers are known for making the best decisions.
- The faster you make decisions, the better, but not if you're making the wrong decisions. You should be taking whatever time you need to make a good decision, but no more and no less. If you don't take enough time, you'll be guessing, not deciding, and if you take too much time, you'll be wishing you had decided when you should have.

- You don't have to know everything to decide something. You need to know the costs involved, the risks, the benefits, the consequences, and the alternatives, but you don't need to know everything about everything in order to decide. You'll never know everything and you'll never be 100% sure of anything, but, then, you don't have to. You only have to know enough.

- If you can't explain your decisions, you shouldn't be making them. Not that you have to explain all your decisions, mind you. But you should be able to explain them if you had to. Your decisions should never be made based only on the silly notion that "it seemed like the thing to do," and they should never be made, "just because." Decisions made "just because" are just bad decisions.

- If you're not in a clear mind to make decisions, you shouldn't be making them. When you're sick, tired, angry, rushed, pressured, distracted, or under the influence, you're not in a clear mind. If you make decisions anyway, you'll regret them later on.

- You can't please everyone with your decisions. You never will, and fortunately, you don't have to. What's good for some people is not always good for others, and some people just won't know what's good for them, anyway. Some people won't really care whether something's good for them or not; they won't be happy with your decision no matter what it is. That's just the way they are. And whether they're pleased or not, most people will eventually get used to just about anything.

- The best decision makers are quicker to make decisions than to change them, but willing to change quickly if it becomes necessary. Making decisions quickly is usually taken to be an indication of decisiveness, which is a good thing; not changing decisions quickly when they should be changed is usually taken to be an indication of stubbornness, or even stupidity, which, obviously, is not a good thing.

Solving your own problems

If you choose to let your boss solve your problems for you, you will never learn how to solve your own problems, and your boss will never forgive you for taking up so much of his time. Bosses don't mind solving problems. Its part of what they get paid to do. What they don't like is having problems dumped on them that someone else could be and should be solving for themselves. Your best problem solvers do the following:

- They don't think of problems as problems, but as challenges, or opportunities to find solutions. They relish the opportunity.
- They have a positive, "can do" attitude. For them, every problem has a solution. If the problem is a difficult one, they tell themselves that it may be difficult, but it's possible, unlike negative thinkers who tell themselves that it may be possible, but it's too difficult. The difference is huge.
- They don't solve a problem unless they're sure it's a problem. It's a problem to them if "what

is" is not "what it should be." It's not a problem just because they don't like it or someone says it's a problem.

- They don't bother solving problems that someone else should be solving. If someone else has the authority, the responsibility, or the expertise to solve the problem, or could benefit greatly by solving it, they let that person solve it, unless, of course, they're asked by that person to help.

- They never wait for a problem to solve itself, knowing that problems left alone almost always go from bad to worse.

- They look for solutions, not faults, knowing full well that it's far more important to know who will be responsible for solving the problem as opposed to knowing who was responsible for causing it. They see, in other words, people as part of the solution, and not part of the problem.

- They look for simple solutions first, knowing that simple solutions are often overlooked because they are so simple, and knowing, too, that simple solutions are often the best solutions.

- They focus on finding the cause of the problem, and not just its symptoms. Eliminating symptoms of a problem, they understand, only allows the problem to resurface at a later time.

- They're not afraid to ask for help. As long as they know that they've at least tried, it no longer matters to them who solves the problem, only that the problem be solved.

- They accept the fact that if a problem can't be solved, they can always learn to live with it.

To every problem under the sun,
there is a remedy or there is none
If there is one, then hurry and find it;
if there is none, then never mind it.—Anonymous

Accepting responsibility for yourself is no small matter, but it's a matter you must undertake. As you move forward, try to remember what could be the ten most important two letter words you'll ever hear—

IF IT IS TO BE, IT IS UP TO ME.

SUMMARY

- To enjoy the privilege of working, you must accept the responsibility that comes with it.
- You are responsible for most of what happens to you, and will be held responsible for much of the rest.
- Being first at anything is always worth something.
- Successful workers simply make better choices than not so successful workers.
- Excuses are nothing more than lies you tell yourself.
- Mistakes are never as important as the manner in which they are handled.
- If you always depend on others to make your decisions and solve your problems, you will always be dependent on others.

<u>Assignments:</u>

1. Look at the list of suggested goals, select one for yourself, and start putting together a plan for achieving it. Keep you plan simple by just listing the two or three most important things you could do to help you achieve your goal.
2. Look at the Top Ten Classic Excuses, and count how many you have used. If you've used any, even one, stop using it now! If you don't count any, look at the list again, and this time, stop making excuses for the excuses you make.

Lesson Six: Making a Commitment to Success

Objectives:

1. To appreciate why success must be earned.
2. To learn how to earn more money.
3. To learn how to get promoted.
4. To learn how to gain respect.

When your work is done, for all to see, what will people say about it? Will they call you a success? And what about you, will you consider yourself a success? Will you have the money, the responsibility, and the respect you want? If you have these things, will it be said that you had earned them?

I hope you succeed, and I hope your success will have been earned, because some things, like money, responsibility, respect, and success, if not earned, are not worth having.

Sometimes, people are paid more or get promoted in spite of themselves, perhaps out of luck, favoritism, nepotism, sabotage, or office politics. For them, there is no respect. They will be resented, even mocked, for having what they shouldn't have. Their "success" will be short lived, and they will get little, if any, satisfaction from what they have. They will soon learn what others before them have learned, that those who succeed in spite of themselves eventually fail because of themselves. They will come to realize that if there's no satisfaction from it, it's not real success.

Most people want to succeed, but few are willing to work for it. Some wish for success, waiting and hoping to get lucky, to be in the right place at the right time, to win the lottery, marry the boss's daughter, or get discovered by a Hollywood talent scout. Rarely do these things bring success to anyone, and even if they did, it would not be a real and lasting success. And trust me; if you don't have that million dollar movie contract by now, you're not going to get it any time soon.

Forget about this stuff. You can't succeed by wishing for it, you succeed by working for it. Focus on your job, and work to be successful at it. Make a commitment to succeed—be willing to do as much as you can, and not satisfied by doing as little as you can.

It's frustrating to managers, co-workers, and customers alike when workers are more interested in what they can get away with than in what they can do. It's this frustration that gives managers ulcers, convinces co-workers to quit, and drives customers to do business elsewhere. It's frustrating also in that most of these workers have no idea how frustrating they can be. In their own minds, they're doing just fine. They see themselves as being overworked and underpaid. If anything, they're being under worked and overpaid.

The greatest frustration is that every one of these workers is capable of doing better, is capable of having the money, the responsibility, the respect, and the success, and all they have to do is turn wishing into working.

Mike Jacobs

How not to succeed

Wishing won't make it so, and neither will showing up, making promises, staying busy, doing just enough, being in the right place, being a nice person, or being in need.

You won't succeed just by showing up at work. Some workers show up all the time, but do little else while there. Some are actually quite adept at finding ways to accomplish nothing, which is not such an easy thing to do. As Leslie Nielson said, "Doing nothing is very hard to do—you never know when you're finished."

Now you might think that if you're punching a time clock, you are getting paid just for showing up. Well, you'd only be partially correct, though, because except for the minimum wage law, there's no law that tells your employer how much they have to pay you, and for how long. If, in between the times you punch in and punch out, you do very little, they won't be paying you very much and it won't be for very long.

Yes, the hours you put in are important, but not as important as the effort you put into those hours and the results you get out. When your performance is evaluated, the hours you are working will count far less than the effort you are making and the results you are getting.

You could put in twelve hours a day, every day, but if you're not making the effort and not getting the results, you won't be getting the money, the promotions, or the respect you want. As a matter of fact, if you're putting in twelve hours a day and not even making an effort, you're cheating your employer. Pray they don't find out.

You won't succeed just by promising that you will. Promise and potential will only take you so far. Sooner or later, your employer will want to see not what you can do, but what you have done. As someone once remarked, "People will judge you by your actions, not your intentions. You may have a heart of gold, but so does a hard boiled egg."

You won't succeed just by staying busy. Running around like a chicken without a head, wasting time, and working on meaningless tasks will get you nowhere. No matter how much time you spend on meaningless tasks, and no matter how well you do them, when all is said and done, they're still meaningless.

You won't succeed just by doing enough. In a recent survey, 50% of workers admitted that they were only doing enough work not to get fired. There's two problems with this idea—you can never really be sure that you've done enough, and in this ever changing workplace, what's enough now may not be enough tomorrow. Of course, there could be a third problem if your employer decides that enough is enough.

Memo to all Employees

As a result of input from our employees, we are pleased to announce the implementation of a new and improved employee incentive program based on performance, to be effective immediately, and to be known as the "Do a Good Job and We'll Let You Keep It" program. The following guidelines will be used to determine your level of performance:

Level one: You do what we expect you to do.
Level two: You do what we tell you to do.
Level three: You do what we say and not as we do. Management.

Note: Getting to keep your job is a good thing.

Mike Jacobs

You won't succeed just by being in the right place at the right time. This is the hope of wishful thinkers everywhere. In truth, it rarely happens. People who find themselves "in the right place at the right time" are rarely surprised to be there because it's their hard work and preparation that put them there.

You won't succeed just by being a nice person or just by having a desire or a need to succeed. If your employer were to give you and your co-workers whatever you wanted or needed, it would soon find itself out of things to give away and shortly thereafter, out of business. And if they paid you or promoted you based on how nice you were, they'd also go broke because you would be, without a doubt, the nicest son of a gun that ever lived. Sainthood would be in your future.

A good day's work and then some

DID YOU KNOW? In a recent survey, 73% of workers said they were less motivated today than they used to be, and 84% admitted that they could be performing better if they wanted to.

Why? What could possibly prevent anyone from not wanting to do better? It's those seven reasons we discussed in lesson five for the reluctance of workers to make good choices, choices like wanting to do better.

Without a doubt, the most important of those seven reasons is the lack of information. It's not that workers don't want to do better; it's just that they don't know how to do better. *Working 101* will show you how.

The "how" is simple—you come to work, and while you're there, you put in a good day's work and then some. You work hard and you work smart. You start working when you punch in and you don't stop working until you punch out. You do this no matter what your job is, no matter how much you're getting paid to do it, and no matter how you feel about the job. You do this every day you go to work. I'll explain further:

1. You can't do a good job if you're not there to do it. Duh!
2. Working hard doesn't mean working yourself to death. It's not going to kill you. As Lord Stanley observed, "I doubt if hard work, steadily and regularly carried on, ever yet hurt anybody." Actually, it's good for you.
3. It's not really hard when you're working smart, when you're making all the right choices about how to do your work. So, there's really no need to "work like a dog," as the old expression goes. (I've long wondered where this expression came from. For the record, I've been watching my dog for some time now, and I've yet to see him do anything that even remotely resembles work.)
4. Working from punch in to punch out doesn't mean you have to work like a robot. You can still take your breaks, do a little socializing, have a little fun, and smoke 'em if you have 'em. Don't overdo it, though, or some day, you just might get replaced by a robot.
5. It doesn't matter what you're getting paid. You took the job knowing what it paid, and now that you're cashing those paychecks, you're obligated to earn them. If you don't want to do that, I'm sure your boss will have no trouble finding someone who will.

6. You can't just pick and choose which tasks you want to do well; you must do them all well. You can't just say, "I don't like doing this," "I'm bored doing that," "I'd rather be doing something else," or, "I don't think this is important enough to be doing." Even if you do dislike it, or it is boring, or you would rather be doing something else, or it isn't that important to you, you still should be doing it to the best of your ability.

7. You can't work hard and smart once in a while. Being good once in a while is never good enough. You can't do as some workers do, and give 100%—12% on Monday, 20% on Tuesday, 30% on Wednesday, 33% on Thursday, and maybe 5% on Friday. TGIF.

Hard work spotlights the character of people: some turn up their sleeves, some turn up their noses, and some don't turn up at all.—Sam Ewig

What about you? Do you have character, or are you just another character?

Going the extra mile

A good day's work will get you a good day's pay, but you might want more. This is where the "and then some" comes in. This is where you stop doing just enough and start doing more than enough. This is where you do what your boss expects you to do, and then you do more. If you want more, you do more.

Many workers have a hard enough time doing the expected, let alone doing more. Still, they sincerely believe they are being underpaid. In a survey conducted in 2000, a whopping 64% of workers felt they were being underpaid for what they did. That, for them, was reason enough not to do more.

Then, of course, there are workers who won't do any more than the expected because they don't want their bosses to expect even more. They just want to put in their eight hours and be left alone. They're perfectly content to be ordinary workers.

Ordinary won't cut it anymore! In this dynamic, ever changing, highly competitive, customer driven, global economy, ordinary workers who want to be left alone will be left behind. There'll be a place for them in this economy, but it won't be a very nice place to be.

If you want to rise above the ordinary, you must be willing to go the "extra mile," to do all the little extra things that added together make one big difference. And when you go that extra mile, you graduate from the ordinary to the extraordinary.

It's not that hard to do. How hard could it be to help a co-worker without having to be asked or assist a customer even though it's not your department? How hard could it be to put in a little overtime so you can finish your work or thank a co-worker for doing a good job? How hard? Not hard at all. And there are so many little things you can do that would mean so much to so many people.

Here's the thing—they must be done without having to be asked, or if you're asked, without any hesitation, and without any expectation on your part of being rewarded for doing them. (Do not fear; the rewards will come.)

Napoleon Hill, the famous motivational speaker, understood well the importance of going the extra mile. He wrote,

It gives one the only logical reason for asking for increased compensation. If a man performs no more service than that for which he is being paid, then obviously, he is receiving all the pay to which he is entitled. He must render as much service as that for which he is being paid, in order to hold his job, or to maintain his source of income, regardless of how he earns it...But he has the privilege always of rendering an overplus of service as a means of accumulating a reserve credit of goodwill, and to provide a just reason for demanding more pay, a better position, or both. Every position based upon a salary or wages provides one with an opportunity to advance himself by the application of this principle, and it's important to note that the American system of free enterprise is operated on the basis of providing every worker in industry with a proper incentive to apply the principle...In America, anyone may earn a living without the habit of going the extra mile. And many do just that, but economic security and the luxuries available under the great American way of life are available only to the individual who makes this principle a part of his philosophy of life and lives by it as a matter of daily habit.

You have a decision to make—do you want to eke out a living, barely surviving from paycheck to paycheck, and burying yourself in debt, or do you want to obtain the "economic security and the luxuries available under the great American way of life?" Well, what do you want?

The highest reward that God gives us for good work is the ability to do better work.—Elbert Hubbard

Is it money you want?

If you've ever wondered why a dollar won't do as much today as it used to do, it's because people won't do as much today for a dollar as they used to do.—Anonymous

Some would take exception to that statement. They would point to the fact that workers are more productive today than ever before. They are, but then, they should be, given advances in technology and a few other factors that have contributed to increased productivity, as we shall discuss in lesson sixteen.

And not only that, according to the U.S. Department of Labor, while productivity has been increasing, wages and benefits have increased three times as fast. As comedian Joey Adams joked, "People are still willing to do an honest day's work. The trouble is they want a week's pay for it." For some of the workers I have witnessed, "… willing to do an honest day's work," is a bit of a stretch.

DID YOU KNOW? The average wage in America is now around $23.00 an hour. The value of benefits was estimated to be between 25% and 35% of wages. Not bad, until you realize that most workers are under the average, not over it. Women, for comparable jobs, earn about 81% of what men earn, up from about 59% in 1970. That's better than it was, but not as good as it should be.

How much are you being paid? Is it enough to meet your needs? If it isn't enough, what are you going to do about it? What can you do?

- You can shop at your local "money store."

Mike Jacobs

- You can pick some money off the money tree that's growing in your backyard next to that oil well.
- You can go down to your local bank and ask for some.
- You can audition for "American Idol."
- You can stand on a corner and sell pencils.
- You can ask me for some.
- You can realize that you're not going to get more money from any of these sources, and that you'll have to get it from work. SO…
- You can get a better paying job.
- You can moonlight at a second job.
- You can work overtime.
- You can work harder and smarter.

Getting a better paying job is always an option, but it's not always easy to do. (See lesson two if this is what you want to do.) Holding down two or more jobs is another option, and millions of people do it, some because they want to, but most because they have to. The problem with this option is that it cuts into your leisure time, wears you down, and affects your performance at your primary job. Working overtime can have the very same effects, and is risky because you're at the mercy of your employer who decides when overtime is needed and whether or not it will be approved.

Your best option is, as you would expect, to do a better job and earn more money. (See lesson twelve for more specifics on earning more money.)

Paycheck 101

I don't know of too many workers who would not like to earn more money, or of too many who are eager to earn less. If you're among the vast majority who would like to make more money, then listen up.

The first thing you should understand is how your wages are determined by your employer. We already know it's not because you show up at work, stay busy, or have tons of potential, and as we both know, it's not because you're the nicest or most attractive person on the face of this earth.

I take that back. You're marvelous, and I'm awed by your good looks and good nature. I was just trying to make a point, that none of these things have anything to do with how much you make. Of course, there are always a few bosses foolish enough to pay someone more solely because that person is nice or attractive. Most bosses, fortunately, are not interested in being sued for discrimination or replaced by a smarter boss.

What if you can prove to your boss that you really need more money, will you get more then? Not likely. If you need more money, that's your problem, not your boss's. As we said earlier, if your employer were to pay you according to your needs, it would soon find itself out of funds. And yes, there are those few bosses who out of a need to be liked or a sincere concern for your problems, will pay you more, but fewer and fewer bosses are doing this anymore because they're learning that to manage out of sympathy is to find oneself out of work.

This is what they'll pay you—only what they have to, and only what they can afford. They'll pay you as little as they can, provided it's enough to get you to take the job in the first place and keep you from leaving (unless they want you to leave.) Market conditions, such as competitors' wages and availability of workers, will help to determine what that will be. If they can get away with paying you minimum wages, they will. After all, why should they pay you more if you'll take the job for less? They will, however, pay you more if you are worth it.

Understand that they will pay you more, not because it's good for you, and not because it's the humanitarian thing to do, but because it's good for business. They're not stupid. They know that if they pay you less than what you're worth, they risk losing you to another employer who's willing to pay more; that if they pay you more than what you're worth, they risk spending good money that could better be spent somewhere else. By paying you what you're worth, they risk nothing. They want to be fair, but being fair means being fair to everyone—to you, to your co-workers, to the customers, to the company's investors, and to the company itself.

Here's a question for you—is it good to be paid more than you're worth? It sounds good, but it's not always a good thing. If your boss believes that you are being paid too much, he might put pressure on you to be more productive, and he might, at some point, decide that he could find someone else who could do the same or better for less.

The hygiene factor

What I'm about to tell you could, arguably, be the most important piece of advice you will ever get about how to make more money at work. It is this—the people at work who make more money don't work harder only if they're given more money; they're given more money because they work harder. They don't tell their boss that if he gives them more money, they will do more work; they just do more work without any expectation of getting more money.

In the 1950's, Herzberg introduced his now famous "Two Factor" theory in which he spoke of motivational and hygiene factors, and their influence on performance. Money, he found, was more of a hygiene factor. It was more of a reason to take a job than to perform better at it. The lack of money, if anything, served to lower job performance, but the giving of more money alone, in the absence of some motivational factor such as recognition or advancement, did not serve to improve job performance.

The moral to this little story is simple—you don't need more money to work harder; you need a better attitude about work. As Elbert Hubbard suggested, "Folks who never do any more than what they get paid for, never get paid for any more than what they do." Even if you have some misguided boss who caves in and gives you more to get you to do more, you can rest assured he will never forget what he had to do, and some day, he'll be looking for payback.

Is it responsibility you want?

By working faithfully eight hours a day,
you may eventually get to be a boss,
and work twelve.—Robert Frost

Before you go for that promotion, be sure you really want it and are ready for it. It is a privilege to be promoted, but as with any privilege, it comes with responsibilities. It might involve more work, longer hours, more problems, greater pressures, bigger decisions, and perhaps the greatest responsibility of all, overseeing other workers. As a supervisor, you are no longer judged solely on your own performance; you are judged on the performance of all your employees. This can be a frightening thing.

I advise you that if you're not ready and willing to take on the added responsibilities, don't accept a promotion just because you want the money or you want to impress your boss or your co-workers. You won't impress anyone if you do the job poorly, and if you do the job poorly, the consequences will not be worth the extra money.

I've seen too many people fail after being promoted into positions for which they were not ready, and they failed, not because they were bad workers, but because they were not ready to be good supervisors. They may have been, as workers, the "cream of the crop," but lacking any supervisory skills, they quickly found themselves overwhelmed, and wishing they had their old jobs back. It doesn't take long for cream to go sour.

I've seen some workers get promoted without having demonstrated any skills, supervisory or not. They get promoted in spite of the fact that they don't deserve to get promoted. Sometimes, it's because of luck or timing; sometimes, it's because there's no one else to promote; sometimes, it's because they're good at backstabbing and playing office politics; sometimes, it's because they're related to, or sleeping with, the boss; and sometimes, it's to get them out of the way or fill some quota.

It doesn't matter why they get promoted because the results are always the same. Not having earned their promotions, they get no satisfaction from them, and every day they spend in a job for which they're not qualified, they spend "under the gun." They know they're not qualified; everyone knows. Will their employees listen to them? Probably not. Will their bosses trust them? Definitely not. Will anyone respect them? Not on your life!

These people are like dinosaurs, and just as the dinosaurs before them did, they will soon become extinct. So don't envy them, and please, don't become one of them. Remember this—the only promotion worth having is one that is earned by virtue of one's demonstrated ability to supervise or one's recognized potential to become a good supervisor, and with that potential must come the ability and the willingness to learn.

Getting promoted

Let's say you've decided that the good things about getting promoted outweigh all the bad, and that you do want the promotion. What do you do now? Do you simply wait to see if you get promoted? What do you think? I think not; I think you should be proactive in getting that promotion. I think:

- You should be focusing first on that job you have right now. Get enthusiastic about it, work hard at it, be smart about it, and get as much feedback as possible on how you're doing at it. If you're not enthusiastic now, and you're not doing a good job now, and you're not concerned about how you're doing, why on earth would your boss ever believe it will be any different if you were to be promoted?
- You should tell your boss that you would like to be considered for promotion at some time in the near future. If he doesn't know that you're interested, he may not give you any thought when a promotion opens up.

- You should think about the promotion you want. Think about what you would do if you were in that position and what skills you would need to do it. Then, start doing it. When the opportunity presents itself, start doing some of the things that need to be done by someone in that position. Your boss will start relying on you to do it, and may decide that it makes good sense, since you're already doing the job, to give you the title and the money that goes with it.

- You should stick around when your co-workers have already left for the day or given up on a project. Again, your boss will start relying on you.

- You should learn to see things from your boss's point of view. Bosses have a much broader but less personal view of the workplace. They have to. If you understand where your boss is coming from, he'll want you right there with him.

- You should be helping to train your replacement. If there is no one qualified to replace you at your current job, your boss may hesitate to promote you out of it.

- You should stop worrying about being noticed and getting credit for the work you do. Confucius said, "Do not worry that no one recognizes you; seek to be worthy of recognition." He was right. All that matters is that you do a good job, and that you know it. (FYI, your boss will know.) Bosses are not deaf, dumb, and blind, in spite of what you may believe. Do a good job, but when you do, share the credit with your co-workers. It takes a person of great humility and self confidence to give credit where it's due and share it willingly with others. That's exactly the kind of person employers are looking to promote.

- You should do what you can to help your boss get promoted. What better way to open up a position that you can be promoted into, or to put yourself into position to move up with your boss? Bosses like to surround themselves with people they can count on.

Is it respect you want?

Everyone wants respect. In the workplace, at least, it is more important to be respected than to be liked. Losing respect can be as devastating as losing a job.

You have to earn respect, to get it and to keep it. It's not something you get automatically, just because you have a big, fancy title behind your name, and it's not something you get just because you think you should have it or demand that you get it. Respect is something others give you when they think you deserve it, not when you think so.

There are things you can do that will earn you the respect of others. Be aware that if you don't do these things, you will earn nothing but disrespect.

- **Have some self respect.** Take care of your health and your appearance. Pay close attention to how you dress, how you look, and how you act around others. Carry yourself with dignity, with head up, shoulders back, and a smile on your face. When you meet people, look them straight in the eye and give them a firm handshake. Don't take these suggestions lightly either. They have been proven, time and time again, to have a positive influence on how people respond to you. Think about it; if you don't respect yourself, why should anyone else?

- **Have respect for others.** Don't hold yourself up as being better than anyone else. Everyone deserves respect. A lesser position or a lower wage does not make someone a lesser person than you. How can they respect you if you don't respect them?
- **Do your fair share.** Don't go looking for ways to get out of doing work, leaving your co-workers to pick up the slack. Nobody likes a slacker.
- **Be honest and trustworthy.** Keep in confidence what is brought to you in confidence, and don't make too many promises. When you make them, people expect you to keep them; if you break them, you'll only disappoint those people. By all means, don't make any promises that you can't keep, or have no intention of keeping.
- **Be reliable.** Come to work, and come on time, unless you are sick. At work, don't leave your work area unless you let someone know where you're going. Workers who are never to be found when there's work to be done are not well respected.
- **Do the right thing.** Sometimes, it's tempting to take the easy way out by doing, not what's right, but what's easy or expedient, politically correct, inoffensive to others, or popular. Being success-ful, however, is not about these things; it's not about being liked. It's about being respected. FYI, people who are respected are generally well liked anyway.

- **Don't be a complainer.** Complainers spend more time complaining than they spend working. Ironically, they waste a lot of time complaining, but complain a lot about not having time. While there's nothing wrong with making a legitimate complaint to the right person through the right channels, complainers are quick to complain about anything and everything to anyone and everyone unfortunate enough to come within the sound of their voice. Nobody respects a complainer.
- **Don't whine when someone else does well or brag when you do well.** Nobody respects a sore loser or an overbearing winner. When people do well, be happy for them; when you do well, be humble.
- **Don't gossip.** Don't even listen to it. When you spread rumors, people start thinking, "It takes one to know one," and asking, "What is he saying about me?" When you listen to gossip, people start assuming that you're guilty by association.
- **Learn to say 'NO.'** If you don't know how, people will use you, but they won't respect you. They will borrow your time and your money until you've got nothing left for yourself. If you learn, however, to say no without being rude or arbitrary, they may not like it, but they'll respect you for it, and they'll go find some other poor sucker who can't say no.
- **Be more critical of yourself and less critical of others.** When you're critical of yourself, it makes you a better person; when you criticize others, it makes them feel worse. They're not

going to respect you for doing that to them. Whether you're being critical of yourself or of others, always remember that the real purpose of criticism is to build people up, not tear them down.

- **Know what you're doing and do it well.** It's almost impossible to have respect for someone who has no idea what he's doing, whose answer to everything is, "I really don't know," and whose performance only proves that to be true.

Being successful is not about what you can get away with, but about what you can get done and how well you can do it; it's not about being satisfied with doing as little as you can, but about being willing to do as much as you can.

No man on earth is so happy as the man who loves his work and goes home at night with a contented heart because of a good day's work well done.—John Wanamaker

SUMMARY

- Money, responsibility, and respect must be earned, or they will not be worth having.
- You must do your best regardless of what job you have or how much you get paid for doing it.
- Those who make more money at work don't work harder only if given more money; they make more money because they work harder.
- You don't need more money to work harder; you need a better attitude about work.

- Those who succeed in spite of themselves eventually fail because of themselves.
- Respect is something others will give you if they feel you deserve it; it's not something you can just ask for, demand, or expect because of your position.

Assignments:

1. Make a list of at least three little things you can do tomorrow to either make a co-worker or a customer happy. Do them tomorrow and see what happens.

Lesson Seven:
Service to Others

<u>Objectives:</u>

1. To appreciate the benefits of serving others first.
2. To recognize when you are being selfish.
3. To understand the consequences of being selfish.

No man has ever risen to real stature
until he has found that it is finer to serve
somebody else than it is to serve himself.—Woodrow Wilson

Most workers have not yet "risen to any real stature" because they have not yet realized that by serving themselves first, they serve no one, including themselves, but by serving others first, they serve everyone, including themselves.

It's not very difficult to find acts of selfishness in the workplace. Many workers do selfish things without knowing that they're doing them, without realizing that they're being selfish, and without understanding the harm they're doing to themselves and those around them. And make no mistake about it, there is harm being done—

- Feelings are being hurt.
- Resentments are being created.

- Friendships are being lost.
- Cooperation is ending.
- Team objectives are not being met.

The company president was addressing the plant employees—'I know that you've all heard that we're going to be automated, and you're worried that these robots are going to take over your jobs. Well, I'm happy to tell you that not only will no one be let go, but you will only be required to work one day a week for a full week's pay. That's right; you only have to work on Wednesdays.' At that, an employee shouts out from the back of the room. 'Every Wednesday?-Bill Dana and Dr. Lawrence Peters

Okay, maybe it's not a true story, but, from what I've seen, it could be. It probably happens all the time. In fact, I wouldn't be surprised to hear another employee shouting out, "Why Wednesdays? Why can't it be Thursdays? Wednesdays are my bowling nights, and without me, they can't win."

It's funny, but it's not. People who are self serving, or selfish, are not funny. Nor are they ever happy. With their "what's in it for me?" attitude, no matter what you do for them, whether that is to praise them, help them, or pay them more, it will never be good enough. They will always want to know, "What have you done for me lately?"

Selfish vs. selfless

There is a huge difference between the selfish workers who look only to serve themselves and the selfless workers who look for ways to serve others. Let's compare the two—

- Selfish workers like to get even; selfless workers like to get along. (You can't get ahead by getting even, but you can get ahead by getting along.)
- Selfish workers don't like to be interrupted, especially when they're on a break; selfless workers don't mind being interrupted, even when they're on a break.
- Selfish workers think nothing of wasting time; selfless workers don't think about wasting time.
- Selfish workers reject criticism if they don't like what is being said or who is saying it; selfless workers accept criticism no matter what is being said or who is saying it. (You need to know how you're doing, whether that's good or bad.)
- Selfish workers call in sick whenever they feel like it; selfless workers call in sick only when they are sick.
- Selfish workers take more break time than they're entitled to; selfless workers take only what they're entitled to.
- Selfish workers make excuses; selfless workers make plans.
- Selfish workers put in overtime only when they need more money; selfless workers put in overtime when the company needs help.
- Selfish workers are never around when you need them; selfless workers are always there when you need them.

- Selfish workers work only where and when they feel like working; selfless workers are willing to work wherever and whenever they're needed.
- Selfish workers resist change when it doesn't suit them; selfless workers embrace change when it suits the company.
- Selfish workers refuse to do more unless paid more; selfless workers do more without any expectation of being paid more.
- Selfish workers look for ways to get out of working; selfless workers look for work to do.
- Selfish workers like to ask, "Why should I help?" Selfless workers ask, "How can I help?"
- Selfish workers finish their work when they want to finish it; selfless workers finish their work when it needs to be finished.
- Selfish workers will do some tasks poorly, on purpose, if they are tasks they don't like doing; selfless workers do all tasks well whether they like doing them or not.
- Selfish workers will get into arguments just for the sake of arguing; selfless workers will avoid arguments for the sake of harmony.
- Selfish workers will never be satisfied, regardless of how much you do for them; selfless workers will always be satisfied, regardless of how little you do for them.
- Selfish workers are careless with the company's money; selfless workers are careful with it.
- Selfish workers are dissatisfied, disgruntled, and disinterested; selfless workers are happy and successful.

Acts of selfishness can be seen everywhere, and heard too—"They don't pay me enough," "there's too much work to do," "there's not enough time," "thirty minutes isn't enough time for lunch," "sixty minutes isn't enough time for lunch," "it's not my job," "it's not my fault," "it's not my problem."

They're like spoiled brats, always whining about something. It's always either too much of this or not enough of that, but never just enough to make them happy. It makes you just want to throw your hands up and say, "enough already."

> Of all the influences which cause man to do wrong, selfishness is surely the strongest.—William R. Bradford

To be selfish is to be foolish. It makes absolutely no sense to choose selfishness over selflessness. You've got to understand that when you're rejecting criticism, you're rejecting help; when you're wasting time, you're missing out on opportunities to be productive; when you're resisting change, you're making yourself obsolete; when you're making excuses, you're keeping problems from being resolved; when you're never around when you're needed, you're not going to be needed for long; when you're careless with the company's money, you're throwing away money that might someday have been yours; when you won't do more unless you're paid more, you won't get paid any more; when you do poorly the tasks you don't like, you may never get to do the tasks you do like; and when you're being selfish, you're being foolish!

If you really want to serve yourself, you must focus your attention on serving others first. It does sound strange, but it's true. It is, as the Bible tells us, better to give than to receive. In his book, The Seven Laws of Success, Deepak Chopra helps to explain why. He writes of the Law of Giving and the Law of Karma—

The Law of Giving teaches us that "the universe operates through dynamic exchange…giving and receiving are different aspects of the flow of energy in the universe…and in our willingness to give that which we seek, we keep the abundance of the universe circulating in our lives."

The Law of Karma teaches us that "every action generates a flow of energy that returns to us in a like kind…what we sow is what we reap…and when we choose actions that bring happiness and success to others, the fruit of our karma is happiness and success."

In other words, when you do something good to other people or give something to them, you set into motion a series of events that eventually brings something good back to you, and this series of events is interrupted only by acts of selfishness. In effect, you get back what you give out, good or bad.

Service to others is critical to your success. In the next three lessons, we will take a closer look at this. In lesson eight, we will discuss service to your customers; in lesson nine, service to your co-workers; and in lesson ten, service to your employer.

SUMMARY

- To serve yourself, you must first serve others.
- Selfishness is foolishness.
- Selfishness hurts you, and it hurts others too.
- You get back what you give out.

Assignments:

1. Reread the section comparing acts of selfish-ness with acts of selflessness. Make a list of all the selfish things you have done. If you're still doing them, stop.
2. Find a co-worker who you don't get along with. Make a point of doing something nice to or for him at least once a day for the next five days. See what happens.

Lesson Eight:
Serving Your Customers

Objectives:

1. To appreciate your customers.
2. To understand your role in bringing in new customers and keeping existing customers.
3. To learn what it takes to satisfy customers.

Without customers who want or need products or services, there would be no need for businesses that provide those products and services, and without those businesses, there would be no jobs for you or anyone else to work

If a business wants to succeed, and I can't imagine why it wouldn't, it must attract customers to it, convince them to purchase goods and services from it, and make them happy so they'll keep coming back to purchase more. The more customers, the better.

It's relatively easy to attract customers to a business. Through advertising, giveaways, sales promotions, discounts, word of mouth, and good old fashioned curiosity, lots of people can be drawn in. This is good for business, but it can also be expensive. If those customers don't make enough purchases or don't come back to make more, the expense may not be worth it.

Customers can just as easily be driven from a business as they can be drawn to it. Poor service, shoddy products, competition, and once again, curiosity, can drive them away.

DID YOU KNOW? A recent study by the Small Business Association found that 68% of customers listed poor service or worker indifference as their reason for leaving a particular business, as compared to only 14% for product dissatisfaction, 9% because of price, 5% because of a friend's recommendation, 3% because of a move, and 1% because of death. (How did that 1% participate in the study? That's what I want to know.)

DID YOU KNOW? The Small Business Administration also found that, on the average, a customer who is dissatisfied will tell from eight to sixteen other people why he is dissatisfied.

The real key to the success of any business lies with the customers who keep coming back, not because of advertising or promotional gimmicks, but because they like doing business there. And, the real key to whether or not they like doing business there lies in the employees of the business.

Getting customers to keep coming back is not as easy as getting them to first come in. All of the advertising, promotions, discounts, and giveaways will mean nothing if their shopping experience is a bad experience.

You must understand that when people shop, they're looking for three basic things—quality, price, and service. Quality and price are important, but not as important as service. People will compromise on quality if they get a better price, and they'll compromise on price if they get a better quality, but they'll almost never compromise on service. A quality product at a good price will not matter if the service is poor. Nobody likes to be treated poorly.

Are you starting to see how important you are? If the key to getting "repeat" business is you, and repeat business is the key to your employer's success, then you are the key to your employer's success. By your actions, its fate will be determined.

When it comes to helping customers, all workers go out of their way, some go out of their way to please their customers and some go out of their way to avoid them. You'd be surprised how many workers will go out of their way to avoid customers, as if they had the plague or something. You'd think they would know better.

But they don't; they don't realize that customers have only so much money to spend, and that there are a whole lot of businesses out there competing for that money. They don't understand that if they can't make customers feel like they're spending their hard earned money wisely, somebody else most certainly will.

Do you know what they call workers who are responsible for driving customers away? They call them "former employees." Do you know what they call workers who are responsible for drawing customers back? They call them something much nicer, such as "employee of the month," or "our new manager."

Does your boss know what to call you? You bet. He sees the customer satisfaction surveys; he reads the letters of appreciation; he hears the complaints; he counts the customers coming in and the customers going out; and, he can see what you're doing with his own two eyes. He knows how you're treating the customers, and he knows what the customers are thinking. He knows more than you think he knows, and why shouldn't he? They're his customers too.

Beyond customer service

"Customer service" is one of those big catch phrases you hear all the time. Everywhere you look, some business is mounting a customer service campaign, with donuts, balloons, and silly little buttons that read, "Smile," "We care," "We love our customers," "Whatever it takes," "If I don't say thank you, it's free," or "V.I.C.," which stands for Very Important Customer. Every time you turn around, there's another book about customer service or another consultant who's more than willing to share his expertise, for a price, of course.

Give me a break. Has service gotten any better? You tell me, because I don't see it. And do you want to know why it hasn't gotten better? Because you can't change a worker's attitude by sticking a little button on his shirt or by insisting that he be nice to his customers. Workers shouldn't have to be told to be nice, they should choose, of their own free will, to be nice.

I'll tell you something else that bothers me; it's the fact that it's really not enough anymore to just provide customer service. We should be moving beyond customer service to customer satisfaction. There is a big difference between the two—you can serve a customer, but you can do it with a smile or a frown, with enthusiasm or indifference, with commitment or detachment. You can serve the customer because you "want to" or because someone else tells you that you "have to." Service with a smile is not always good service!

Customer satisfaction is not just about serving your customers, it's about serving them well; it's about going out of your way to please your customers all of the time; it's about appreciating how important they really are to you, and showing that appreciation; and it's about believing that whatever you do for them, you can never do enough.

Read that paragraph again, because it bears repeating. Your job may depend on whether or not you take what it says to heart.

The ten golden rules of customer satisfaction

1. Be thankful for their business.
2. Know what they want.
3. Look for opportunities to serve them.
4. When they need help, make it your top priority.
5. Always respond promptly and courteously.
6. Listen to them even when they're angry.
7. Listen to them even when they're being rude or obnoxious.
8. Admit when you're wrong.
9. When they're wrong, let it go.
10. Don't complain to them or in front of them.

Rule #1: Be thankful for their business. Without it, you might not have a job; because of it, you do, and you get paid for doing it too; and, the more business you help to bring in, the more you will be paid.

So, here is this customer, this person who has this money to spend, money that he might have worked hard to earn, and now, he's thinking about spending it where you work. Remember, he has other options; he can spend his money somewhere else if he wants to. Instead, he has chosen to come to you, and has, in effect, given you an opportunity to be of service.

This is your opportunity, your customer. Take this opportunity to show your customer how much you appreciate his business, to treat him with the utmost respect, to give him your undivided attention, to make him your number one priority, and to go out of your way to assist him. Treat your customer as you would want someone to treat you.

There's too much riding on this not to take this opportunity seriously. If you can satisfy your customers, make them feel like they made the right choice in coming to you, you'll be greatly rewarded for it, but if, on the other hand, you make them regret their decision to come, you'll greatly regret it too. Just think, for example, of all the workers who depend on tips who miss out on the opportunities to make bigger tips just by treating their customers better. How foolish is that?

Rule #2: Know what they want. Who is this customer of yours? What do you know about him? What does he want? What does he need? And, what does all this matter to you?

It matters because the more you know about your customers, the better able you will be to serve them well. How, on the other hand, could you possibly give them what they want or what they need if you don't know what that is? By chance, perhaps? Are those the kind of odds you want working for you? I hope not.

It's important that you know your customers and that you know your products and services so you can tailor your products and services to meet their needs and their desires. That's how "the deal is sealed." But if you don't know what your customers want, or if, worse still, you don't care what they want, and you care only about sealing that deal, you might get it sealed if you're lucky, but for your customers, it will be a raw deal. You can fool them once, but they won't be back again.

Here's another question for you—do you know what your customers don't want? You should know that too. Why? Because if they don't want something, you shouldn't be offering it to them; if they don't like having something done, you shouldn't be doing it. You don't want to disappoint them or make them mad. They're not going to be satisfied customers if they're dissatisfied!

Now listen carefully to what I'm about to say—you should be thankful when your customers come to you with complaints. Yes, you read that correctly. You should be thankful because if they're not happy, it's better that they complain to you about it, than complain to someone else about you. By complaining to you, they're giving you a heads up on how to improve your products or services, and how to improve your own performance. If, instead, they just took their business elsewhere, you'd be losing both a customer and an opportunity to improve.

Before we go to rule #3, I want you to understand that today, it is even more critical that you heed this advice. Consumers have changed. Whereas once upon a time, they expected and even accepted poor service, they no longer will. The baby boomers are all grown up now, and they have lots of money to spend, as do their kids. They've worked hard to earn their money, and they're willing to spend it, but they're not going to fork it up to just anyone. They're fully aware of all the options they have, and very knowledgeable about those options.

They have more options today than ever before, as more businesses are competing for their dollars, and because of the Internet, more businesses are becoming accessible to them. They don't even have to leave home to go shopping anymore.

They have more information today than ever before. Once again, the Internet has made it possible for them to know what products and services are available to them. Some of these consumers have so much information that they know the products and services better than the people who are selling them.

With all this money and information, and all of the options available to them, do you think they're going to be more particular, more demanding, and more selective than ever before? You bet! Do you think it would be wise for you to know what they want, and to know, also, what you have to give them? You bet!

Rule #3: Look for opportunities to serve them. We know there are workers who go out of their way to avoid customers, who when they see a customer coming, walk away or pretend to be busy. To these workers, customers are nothing but interruptions in their workday.

As Ken Blanchard wrote, "A customer is not an interruption of our work; he is the purpose of it. We are not doing a favor by serving him…He is doing us a favor by giving us the opportunity to do so."

Remember, your customers are not interrupting you; they are giving you an opportunity to be of service to them, an opportunity for you to succeed. So the next time a customer approaches you, instead of thinking, "Oh great, what does he want now?" think, "Great, here's my opportunity to shine." Instead of saying, "Why should I help?" say, "How can I help?"

P.S. You don't have to wait for a customer to ask for help. Some of them never will, even if they need it.

Rule #4: When they need help, make it your top priority. Are you busy? Working on a project? Filling out a report? Talking to a co-worker? Surfing the Internet? Taking a break? Taking a nap? Well, I have news for you, no matter what you're doing, if a customer needs help, you need to help the customer; you need to stop doing whatever you're doing, and help the customer, or help to get them the help they need. Nothing is more important than helping a customer.

Never, ever, ignore a customer, because nobody likes to be ignored. Nobody likes to wait at the counter while you're talking on the phone; nobody likes to wait at the checkout stand while you find out what a co-worker is doing over the weekend; nobody likes to sit around waiting for repair work to be done while the repairman eats his lunch. I'm not saying that you shouldn't talk on the phone or chat with your co-workers or have your lunch; I am saying that you should at the very least, acknowledge the customer's existence, promise to get to him as soon as you can, and make sure that you do. That's the least you can do, because unless there's some very good reason why you can't do it, you should stop whatever you're doing immediately, and help your customer.

One more thing on this rule—all customers are your customers, always, no matter how long you've been working there, no matter which department you're working in, and no matter what it says in your job description. There is no good excuse not to help a customer. So, "it's not my department," or "I'm new here," are unacceptable. Even if it isn't your department or you are new, you can still try to help the customer or get someone else who can help. Customers will always appreciate your efforts, even if you can't be of any real help.

When you do stop to help a customer, give him your undivided attention. Make him feel as though he's the sole purpose for you being there. As Stephen Lundin suggested in *Fish*, "be present and stay focused on your customer."

Rule #5: Always respond promptly and courteously.
Whatever the customer wants, no matter how rude he

is or how stupid it is, you must respond to it promptly and courteously. You must be sincere in your efforts to resolve any complaints and please the customer.

Problems can be fixed; complaints can be resolved; misunderstandings can be clarified. All can easily be forgiven and forgotten if they are handled promptly and courteously. If, on the other hand, customers with needs or concerns are made to wait and treated with rudeness and disrespect, there may be no forgiveness.

The good thing is that unhappy customers who are treated right soon become happy customers and, as is often the case, may become your best customers. Everyone likes to be treated right.

Rule #6: Listen to them even when they're angry. You need to hear what your customers have to say, even if they're mad, especially if they're mad. You want to defuse that anger, resolve any concerns they may have, and make them happy again. There's a way to do that:

- Let them vent their anger or frustration. Once they get it out of their system, they usually calm down. It will then be easier to talk to them and reason with them. Sometimes, getting it off their chest is all they need to do.
- Don't interrupt them when they're talking. Whenever a customer is talking, that's always a good time for you to be listening. How else can you find out what they're angry about?
- Tell them you understand how they feel, and that you would probably feel the same way if you were in their shoes. Better still, put yourself in their shoes.
- Ask them what they want you to do. Sometimes, they don't really know. They've been too busy

being angry to even think about it. Sometimes, when you ask, they'll realize there's really nothing you can do. And sometimes, they'll tell you.

- Get them what they want. If you can't, either find someone who can, or explain, in a nice way, why you can't. Offer, in that case, some alternative solutions.
- Thank them for letting you know of their concerns, and allowing you to be of service to them. Offer to help again if that ever becomes necessary.

Rule #7: Listen to them even if they're being rude or obnoxious. Some customers go way beyond being angry, they get downright ugly. They can be so rude, nasty, or stupid that it will literally push you to the limits of your patience.

Do not, however, let them push you over the edge. Don't ever say or do anything you might later regret. Even if they deserve to hear it, you don't deserve to get fired for saying it. Even if your boss understands why you said what you said or did what you did, he may still have to fire you for it. That may not seem right to you, but it's not about what's right or wrong, it's about what's good for business.

Now, there are, of course, lines that even customers should not be allowed to cross, and in those cases, a good boss will side with the employee, and ask the customer to leave. Having customers like that is bad for business.

Rule #8: Admit when you're wrong. Anyone can make a mistake; everyone does. As we learned, it's how you handle your mistakes that counts. Your customers will almost always forgive you for making a mistake if you just have the good sense to say, "I'm sorry." When you do, most people will respond by saying something like, "That's okay; it's really not a big deal."

What they won't forgive, though, is an obvious attempt to cover up a mistake that was made, or an attitude from you that says, "What's the big deal?"

Too many workers get overly defensive when a customer tells them that they did something wrong. As I said before, this is something you should be grateful for, not defensive about.

Rule #9: When they're wrong, let it go. Contrary to what all the customer service gurus are teaching you, the customer is not always right. I know there will be some who disagree with me on this, but it's true.

Here's the thing—it doesn't matter if they're right or wrong; all that matters is that if they're right, they're right, and if they're wrong, you still respond as if they were right. You have to believe that your customers are right, at least about something, and that they always have certain rights as customers—

- They have the right to be treated with respect.
- They have the right to be wrong, and still be treated with respect.
- They have the right to be upset.
- They have the right to express their feelings.
- They have the right to get what they want, even if it's not what they need.
- They have the right to have all wrongs done against them made right.

Here's what most of your co-workers believe:

- That the customer is usually wrong.
- That the customer doesn't know right from wrong.

- That what the customer doesn't know won't hurt him.
- That it doesn't matter what the customer says anyway.
- That even if the customer is right, we can never admit it.
- That the customer is rude, so it doesn't matter if he's right.
- That the customer is right...until he can no longer hear what we really think.

Is the customer always right? Who cares? All you need to remember is to let it go.

Rule #10: Don't complain to them or in front of them. When you complain to them, or they overhear you complaining, about being overworked, underpaid, understaffed, unappreciated, and misunderstood, it makes them think about what kind of business this is that would treat people so poorly, and why they should continue to do business there. It's not very reassuring to a customer to learn that "this place is nuts."

Besides, nobody wants to hear about your problems. They've got their own, and if they wanted to listen to someone else's problems, they could easily stay home and watch "Jerry Springer." Now those people have problems.

Satisfy your customers—meet their needs; respect their decisions; consider their feelings; exceed their expectations; appreciate their importance; listen to their concerns; resolve their issues; honor their requests. Do these things, and your customers will come back, and they'll ask for you when they do. And as long as they keep coming back, you will too.

SUMMARY

- Without your customers, you'd be out of a job.
- You, and your co-workers, are the key to your employer's success.
- Customer satisfaction is more than customer service. It is customer service done well, done consistently, and done willingly.
- The ten rules of customer satisfaction should be followed every day.

Assignment:

1. As a consumer, make a note of all the times you are displeased by the service you receive. Think about what the person did that bothered you, and what you would do if you were in his place. Would you do the right thing?

Lesson Nine:
Serving Your Co-workers

<u>Objectives:</u>

1. To understand the relationship between your job and every other job.
2. To learn the meaning of, and the importance of, teamwork.
3. To learn how to get along with your co-workers.

Nobody works alone. You, your boss, and your co-workers are in this thing called work together, for better or for worse, for richer or for poorer, until termination or retirement do you part. You may not kiss each other now.

If you want it to be better, and you're looking to be richer, and you're not quite ready to retire, then you, and they, must learn to set aside all your differences and learn to get along so together, you can succeed.

This is not an option. Whether you like it or not, you need each other. "Every job," wrote Byham and Cox, "has an effect on the job ahead of it and behind it." You depend on them doing their jobs so you can do yours; they depend on you doing your job so they can do theirs. As John C. Maxwell explains, "Every day, in some way, you are part of a team. The question is not 'Will you participate in something that involves others?' The question is, 'Will your involvement with others be meaningful?"

113

What is a team?

What is a team, and what does it mean to you to be on one? A team is a group of people who have been joined together for the purpose of working towards a common goal. Without the common goal, a group of people is a group of people, and nothing more. It is not a team.

For it to be a winning team, all team members must know what the common goal is, must want to achieve it, must acknowledge that it can only be achieved through the combined, cooperative efforts of everyone on the team, and must understand that if the goal is achieved, all team members are to benefit.

The potential benefits of a winning team are many—the work gets done much faster, much easier, and much better, and the act of working, for all team members, gets much more satisfying. The goal is achieved, and all are compensated for it.

Individual efforts are not lost in the shadow of the team's accomplishments. On the contrary, they are made more visible by it. Just look at your favorite team sport for proof of this. How often does the league MVP come from a losing team? Not very often.

Would you like to be on a winning team? Then be prepared to make your contribution to it—

- Know what its common goal is.
- Commit to achieving that goal.
- Work together with your co-workers to achieve it.
- Share the rewards.

Going one on one

If I've heard it once, I've heard it a thousand times—there is no 'I' in 'TEAM.' (Together Everyone Achieves More.) While I do agree that together, everyone achieves more, and I do appreciate the spelling lesson, I have to somewhat disagree with their conclusion. You see, there are lots of I's in TEAM, and they're called Individuals.

Vince Lombardi once said, "The achievements of an organization are the results of the combined effort of each individual." The whole is indeed greater than the sum of its parts, but without those parts, there would be no whole.

I'm not trying to be cute here; I bring this up for a reason, the reason being that if you are to be a good team player, you will have to get along with the individuals who are on the team, in a series of one on one encounters, which, if not handled properly, can be encounters of the worst kind.

DID YOU KNOW? In a survey done in 2000 (which apparently was a very busy year for surveyors), 41% of workers said that they disliked their co-workers; 46% said that they disliked their bosses.

You can never underestimate the power of human stupidity or the frequency with which it occurs. Nor can you ignore the greed, the selfishness, or hatred that is so prevalent today. People can do the dumbest and the cruelest things to each other. Is it any wonder they dislike each other? Getting along with each other can seem like an impossible task when it's difficult enough just getting through the day without killing each other.

Don't you just get tired of hearing people trash each other all day long? "Nobody understands what I have to put up with." "He's so impatient." "Nobody wants to help around here." "You can't talk to anyone in this place." "This place is nuts." "This place is a zoo." "How she ever got to be the boss, I'll never know." "How rude can one person be?" "Am I the only one who does anything around here?" "Why is he still working here?" "What the hell are these people thinking?" "Is she really that ignorant?" "Can you believe what he said?" "Did you see what she was wearing?" "Did you hear about his problem?" "Can you believe the nerve of her talking about me?"

Why don't they just sum it all up by saying, "If it wasn't for my boss, my co-workers, and my customers, I wouldn't mind this job." Wouldn't you like to tell these people to just shut the hell up and get back to work? I know I would. You're not one of these people, are you?

People like this can just suck the life right out of you if you listen to them long enough. It reminds me of that expression, "How can you soar like an eagle when you're cooped up with turkeys?" Well, if you want to soar, you must learn to work with all the turkeys.

You can't ignore these people, because they're not going away any time soon, but, at the same time, you can't continue to put up with their garbage, because it's not good for anyone, not for you, not for them, and not for the team.

It's time, my friend, for you to learn your IPR's.

From ABC's to IPR's

When you were a little kid, you had to learn your ABC's. Now that you're all grown up and going to work, it's time for you to learn your IPR's, which stands for interpersonal relations, and represents the ins and outs, and the do's and don'ts of getting along with other people, in this case, with your co-workers and your boss.

We will begin by talking about your co-workers, and then, because of the special relationship you have with your boss, we will talk about that separately. But first, we must talk about two very important principles, the truth of which you must wholeheartedly accept if these IPR's are going to work. If you can't believe this stuff, you'll never get along with anyone.

The first principle is one which we have already discussed at length. It is the principle of service to others—to serve ourselves, we must first serve others. A spirit of cooperation cannot be built upon acts of selfishness.

The second principle is that of mutual dependence—we need each other (whether we like it or not.) Unless and until you can believe this, you will never be able to trust anyone, to respect anyone, or to get anyone to cooperate with you. Nor will you be able to tolerate all the stupid and cruel things that they do.

I know what you're thinking, that there are some very, very evil people in this world who you could never like, respect, or trust. I would be rather surprised if any of your co-workers were truly evil people. I can assure you that if you look for the good in people, you can usually find some. Sure, for some folks, you may have to look a little harder, but it's there somewhere. Even the "good for nothings" are good for something, if not in your eyes, then in someone else's.

Listen, nobody's perfect. We all screw up from time to time. We all have our issues. "We all have baggage," wrote Bob Rosner, "and we're constantly tripping over each other's stuff...There's so much emotional baggage strewn around the workplace, there's no way to navigate without sustaining bruises. In fact, most of the time, I wonder how anything gets done."

It's the baggage that makes it hard to get anything done, but if we all can learn to get along at work, we can do what the airlines do, and lose our baggage.

The IPR dos and don'ts

Follow the Golden Rule. Treat people as you would want them to treat you. The Bible says, "Do unto others as you would have them do unto you." It doesn't say, "Do unto others before they do unto you," or "Do unto others and then run like the wind." Remember, the Golden Rule is not about getting even, it's about getting along.

Don't judge people; judge their behaviors. There's good and bad in all people of all races, creeds, and colors. To judge them based on who they are or how they look would be unfair to them and to you. You would be running the risk of isolating yourself from people who could help you, support you, inform you, befriend you, or otherwise make your life easier at work.

When they do bad things, keep in mind that everyone has good days and bad days, high points and low. Sometimes, people do things they would not normally do; sometimes, they don't even know what they're doing. The point is that a bad day or a bad behavior does not make a person bad. So, judge their behaviors if you must, but nothing else.

Don't judge behaviors that you don't understand. Things are not always what they seem to be. People may have good reasons for doing what they do, although those reasons might not be so obvious to you. They could be tired, sick, angry, scared, pressured, or misinformed, or they could be responding to something that someone else did to them. Maybe you were that someone.

What looks like inappropriate behavior to you may be quite appropriate given the circumstances. A worker, for instance, who seems to lack ambition, may not be able to see any opportunities; one who never shares ideas with his boss may have a boss who never listens; and another who appears to be insubordinate, may, in fact, be responding appropriately to an unreasonable demand. What appears to be insubordination may actually be good sense and courage.

So, find out their reasons before you judge their behaviors. It will prevent a lot of misunderstanding.

Be willing to compromise. Whenever two or more people have to spend any time together, there will be conflict. If you've ever been married, you know what I'm talking about. Now, married folks, you must remember, chose to spend time together. You chose your job, but you probably didn't choose it so you could be together with your co-workers. You probably didn't know them before you took the job, so you can imagine the conflicts that will follow.

Conflict, contrary to popular belief, is not necessarily a bad thing. If it's handled right, it could lead to progress, and progress is a good thing. It's when conflict is not handled properly that it leads to problems.

Handling conflict properly means being open minded (which is not the same thing as having a hole in your head), being sensitive to feelings and respectful of opinions, being assertive about what you want, and above all, being willing to compromise. You don't have to have it your way all the time. You know where you can go to get that, well, at least some of the time.

Getting along with your co-workers is not about who wins and who loses; it's about everyone winning together. Through compromise and cooperation, this can happen. Without compromise and cooperation, nobody wins. Feelings are hurt, friendships are lost, and misunderstandings become the norm.

Don't compromise on your values. If you believe strongly in something, be it the goodness of man, the power of faith, the value of hard work, the American way of life, or anything else, don't compromise on it. Your values underlie everything you do, so they're too important to compromise on. There are so many other, less important things that happen every day that you can compromise on.

Just for the record, believing strongly in things like the power of evil, the destruction of mankind, or the superiority of one group over another, as far as I'm concerned, is not about values, but about sickness. Those, I would recommend strongly that you compromise on.

Don't argue or lose your temper. NEWSFLASH: If somebody wants to start an argument with you, you're not obligated to finish it! If you refuse to join in, there will be no argument. As the saying goes, "a fire not fueled soon burns out."

What's the point of an argument, anyway? To get someone to change his mind, right? Well, when you argue with someone, they tend to get defensive, which makes them even less willing to change. So, by arguing, you're just wasting your breath. Instead of arguing, take a deep breath, and walk away.

Arguing is a good way to make yourself look foolish, even if you win the argument. Consider the first law of debate, which states, "Never argue with a fool. People might not be able to tell the difference." Even if the person you're arguing with is not a fool, you might both still look foolish.

You need to exercise some self restraint. If someone wants to argue, you don't have to argue too; if someone tries to hurt you by hurling insults at you, you don't have to get insulted, and it doesn't have to hurt; if your boss is "just asking for it" by acting like a jerk, you don't have to give it to him. With your boss, being right will not always protect you from being fired.

Admit when you're wrong. It doesn't take a big person to admit that he's wrong; it takes a person with common sense. If you're wrong, you're wrong, no matter what you believe. Unless you want to continue to be wrong, it only makes sense to make things right. That won't happen until you first admit you were wrong. If what you've said or done has hurt someone, apologize for it, and ask if there is anything you can do to make things right. An apology is, more often than not, all that is needed.

Along the same lines, if someone has hurt you, and is now trying to apologize for it, accept the apology, get over it, and move on. There's very little that any of us could do to each other at work that would be so devastating that work would have to stop, and life as we know it would cease to be.

Be assertive. Not timid, not aggressive, but assertive, so you can let people know how you feel, what you want, and what you need. You don't have to be afraid to ask for what is rightfully yours, for what you deserve, and for what you want. But you ask. You don't beg, you don't demand, you ask.

A timid person keeps his feelings and opinions to himself. He is too shy to ask for what he wants. People tend to pity such persons.

An aggressive person expresses his feelings and opinions freely, even if no one wants to hear them. He doesn't ask for things, he demands them. People tend to resent such persons.

An assertive person is willing to share his feelings and opinions if someone is willing to listen. When he wants something, he either asks for it, or, in a calm, confident manner, lets it be known what he wants. People tend to admire such persons.

So what would you rather be, pitied, resented, or admired?

Don't be a jerk. Don't say or do hurtful things, even if you're just kidding; don't brag when you win or whine when you lose; don't gossip, complain, interrupt, talk too much, be too loud, argue, put people down, or bother co-workers who are trying to work. There are more than enough annoying, life sucking jerks in the workplace already. They don't need one more.

Be nice. It's not that hard to do. You get up in the morning, and you decide—am I going to spend my day making people happy or making them miserable? Once you've made your choice, the rest is easy. How hard could it be to wear a smile, and not a frown, to praise people when they deserve praise, to be grateful when praised by others, or to be thankful for the things they do for you or give to you? How difficult could it be to say something nice to someone, and to not say anything when you don't have anything nice to say?

I'm not asking you to qualify for sainthood. We both know that it's already too late for that. I'm just asking you to be nice, that's all. And not just because it's the nice thing to do, but because it's the wise thing to do. If you want to get along with your co-workers, you can't go around starting arguments, picking fights, holding grudges, badmouthing people, or being rude, obnoxious, ignorant, disruptive, or annoying. You can't be a jerk.

When you don't praise people, they feel unappreciated; when you don't thank them for what they give to you or do for you, they stop giving and doing; when you act like a jerk to them, they want nothing to do with you. How on earth can you get along with people who want nothing to do with you?

Be respectful. Show some respect for all of your co-workers, no matter how they look, how they act, how they dress, how much money they make, or what they do for a living. They're all just trying to make a living and get along, just like you. That alone, earns them the right to be respected.

Mutual respect is the foundation upon which all relationships are built. Each of us deserves to be respected and has to be respectful. For many people, their dignity and self respect is the most important thing they have. If you take that from them, there is no way you will ever get along with them.

Trust others, and be trustworthy. You can't be in all places at all times; you can't know everything there is to know; and you can't do everything that needs to be done. You have to be able to trust others to be where you can't be, to know what you don't know, and to do what you can't do. Remember, you're not in this thing alone, and you can't do it alone either.

The good news is that the more you trust others, the more trustworthy they become. "Trust men," wrote Emerson, "and they will be true to you." On the other hand, if you show people that you don't trust them they will become less trustworthy. Knowing you don't trust them, they'll be more likely to do things to prove you right than to prove you wrong. It sounds odd, but it's true. People will live up to your expectations of them.

Trust them, but let it be a guarded trust, because even the most trustworthy person, given the right temptations, can let you down.

Be the kind of person who others can trust—honest, reliable, sincere, knowledgeable, competent, and selfless. When you say you're going to do something, do it; when you make a promise to someone, keep it; when you're asked to keep something in confidence, keep it in confidence. Don't get involved in telling secrets, spreading rumors, or playing office politics. How many people do you know who trust politicians?

Don't try to change people. If you try, you will almost certainly try in vain. If you want them to change, then you change first. We just saw how you can make people trustworthy by trusting them more. You can just as easily get them to be friendlier by befriending them. As Emerson said, "The only way to have a friend is to be one." And you can make people feel good about themselves by praising them, get them to be more cooperative by cooperating with them, defuse any anger they may have by understanding them, and get them to open up just by listening to them.

You can't just expect them to be trustworthy, ask them to be friendly, insist they feel good about themselves, demand that they cooperate, or ignore their anger and hope that it goes away. It doesn't work that way.

You have a lot more influence than you think you have, and you need to be aware of the effect you have on other people, and it's not always a positive effect. If you're suspicious of people, they will become less trustworthy; if you're rude or insensitive to them, they will become less friendly; if you are always critical of them, they will start to feel bad about themselves; if you're demanding and unwilling to compromise with them, they'll be less willing to cooperate; if you respond to their anger with anger of your own, they will only fight harder.

Use the influence you have to do the right thing, to build people up, and not tear them down. At work, it can make the difference between building up a strong support system for yourself or building up a wall between you and your success.

Be willing to help. Help your co-workers when they need help, whether they ask for it or not, and whether they appreciate it or not. You help because it's the right thing to do, and it's what you would want them to do for you if you needed the help. Even if people are too proud to ask or too ignorant to appreciate, they still may need help, and you still should give it to them.

Just don't get in the habit of doing their work for them on a regular basis. You have your own work to do, and they need to learn how to do theirs.

You do have co-workers who will "dump" on you if you let them. The more you do for these people, the more they'll want you to do. If you're always willing to help, they'll always need help; if you're always willing to solve their problems, they'll always have problems to solve; if you're always willing to cover for them, they'll always be gone; if you're always willing to lend them your time (or you money, for that matter), they'll always be willing and eager to borrow it.

Don't enable these people. You're not doing them any good by doing everything for them. Do, however, help those who are making a real attempt to help themselves. Some day, the shoe may be on the other foot.

Be willing to share. To be a winning team, everyone must contribute to its success. All must share the burden so that all can share the wealth. Supplies must be shared so that everyone has enough; information must be shared so that no one feels left out; blame must be shared so that no one feels guilty; praise must be shared so that everyone feels good. When everything is shared, there will always be more than enough to go around.

Mind your own business. Yes, I'm talking to you. Do your job, and stop wasting your time worrying about what everybody else is doing, unless, of course, it's having some effect on your job. Believe me, if you don't mind your own business, it will never get done.

You don't have to worry, either, about competing with your co-workers or about how your performance compares to theirs. With competition and comparisons, there is always someone who loses, always someone who's hurt. Why do that? It's not like you and your co-workers are on different teams; you're all on the same team.

Do yourself a favor, and if you must compete, compete with yourself. Challenge yourself to do better every day. Use the "one more than you did before" approach if you wish. Just remember that you don't have to be the best, you just have to do your best.

Be more critical of yourself than you are of others. Confucius said, "If a man would be severe toward himself and generous toward others, he would never arouse resentment."

It never ceases to amaze me how many people there are who hate to be criticized, yet are so quick to point out the mistakes of others, and so slow to forget them. Again, don't worry about what others are doing; think about what you're going to do.

Never seek to gain an advantage at someone else's expense. In the game of getting even, nobody gets ahead. If you take advantage of someone, he will resent you for it, and if the opportunity presents itself, he may seek to regain the advantage, at your expense.

Lots of workers engage in office politics, seeking to gain that advantage. As I see it, politics has no place in the workplace. Politics is for people who like to kiss babies and can never give a straight answer to a simple question. In the workplace, questions must be answered, and babies are hard to find.

Do the right thing. There will be times when you'll be forced to make a difficult choice—should you take something that doesn't belong to you? Should you take credit that you don't deserve? Should you make a promise that you can't keep? Should you withhold information to protect a co-worker? Should you turn in a co-worker for something bad they have done? Well, what should you do?

You should do the right thing, even if it's not the easy or the popular thing to do. Remember, this is not a popularity contest. Yes, it's nice to be liked, but at work, it's better to be respected. I, for one, would rather have people respect me for having the courage to do the right thing, than have them like me, yet disrespect me, for "selling out."

But that's just me. We're talking here about you, and the choices you will have to make for yourself. I just hope you choose well.

Exercise your rights responsibly. As an employee, you have certain rights that have been mandated by law. If you are in what is called a "protected class," i.e. minorities, people with disabilities, and persons, like me, who are over forty, you have some additional rights as well.

You should know your rights, and use them, if necessary, to protect yourself, but never use them to gain an unfair advantage, or to excuse yourself from doing a good job. They are rights, mind you, not weapons or excuses. If you want to reap the benefits of work, refer back to lesson six, and learn how to earn it.

For every right you're entitled to, you have to understand, there's a responsibility that goes with it. The right to be judged by your performance only, as an example, is accompanied by the responsibility to perform to the best of your ability; the right to be free from sexual harassment is accompanied by the responsibility to not provoke it; the right to be paid for time lost from a work related injury is accompanied by the responsibility to return to work as soon as you are able.

We all have rights and responsibilities, and if we are to get along with each other, each of us must exercise our rights responsibly and take our responsibilities seriously.

Getting along with your boss

A good boss can do a lot of good things for you. He can make sure you have the supplies, the information, and the training you need; he can offer you support when you need it; he can give you the freedom to use your initiative and the room to make mistakes without fear of reprisal; he can see that you get the raises and the promotions you deserve.

A bad boss, on the other hand, can do a lot of bad things to you. He can hassle you all day long, overload you with work, keep you in the dark about what's going on, criticize you unjustly, and stand in your way of getting those raises and promotions.

Your boss can either make your life easier at work or make it a living hell. And you can do the same to him. It all depends on how the two of you get along. You will get along just fine if you remember your IPR's, the ones we just talked about and the ones we're going to talk about now, which will help you get along better with your boss.

Make your boss look good. Do your job, the way it should be done, and your boss will look good. It's his job to make sure that you are doing your job. If you are, he has done his job well. On the other hand, if you screw up, it reflects poorly on both of you.

Suppose you do screw up, do you think that your boss is going to be a happy camper? Do you think he's going to thank you for making him look bad? I don't think so. I think he's going to pressure you to do better, start looking over your shoulder to see what you're doing, and start jumping down your throat anytime you screw up. Is that what you want? I didn't think so.

Always remember that although you're responsible only for your own actions, your actions have an effect on others.

Ask if you need help. Sometimes, bosses forget to give their employees the help they need. Sometimes, they just get too busy or distracted to remember, but more often than not, they just assume that since you're not asking for help, you don't need it. All you have to do is ask, and most bosses will be more than happy to help.

Your boss should be spending time with you, but if you don't ask, he may not; he should be giving you feedback on how you're doing, but if you don't ask, he may not; he should be letting you know what his expectations are, but if you don't ask, he may not.

Mike Jacobs

There are lots of things bosses should be doing that they're not doing. "Should be," however, doesn't do you any good. Look at expectations, as an example. You can't do what's expected of you if you don't know what's expected. Unless you ask, though, many bosses will not tell you what they expect until after you haven't done it. If you protest by saying, "but you never told me," their answer is likely to be, "but you never asked." Believe me; they'll be quicker to point out your mistake than to point out theirs.

Solve your own problems. Isn't your boss supposed to solve problems? Yes, but he usually has more than enough of them to solve without you bringing him one more. Most bosses, given the choice, would much rather have their employees solve their own problems.

Even if you can't solve the problem, the fact that you tried will be greatly appreciated.

Do what you're told. Unless you're being asked to do something that's illegal, immoral, or hazardous to your health, do what you're asked. Even if you don't like who is asking, how he's asking, or what he's asking you to do, do what you're asked. Even if you're not being asked, but being told, do what you're told. Don't get all worked up about it, and go spouting off about how "it's not my job," or "you're not my boss," or "nobody talks to me like that," or "nobody tells me what to do," unless, of course, you don't mind putting your job on the line.

Let me tell you something, it is your job, he is the boss, he can talk to you like that, and he can tell you what to do. So get over it. If you don't like it, do it anyway, and then, make you complaint at the right time, to the right person, in the right manner.

Speak up, not out. Most bosses, believe it or not, are not too fond of workers who always "yes" them to death.

They prefer agreement, of course, but will welcome disagreement as long as you're not being disagreeable, rude, nasty, and/or insubordinate, and as long as you're keeping the disagreement just between the two of you. It's okay to speak up to your boss, but not out against him.

By all means, say what you have to say, but when all is said and done, if your boss still insists on doing things his way, then do it his way. He is the boss. Do it; do it to the best of your ability; and, do it enthusiastically. If you're not happy about it, keep that to yourself. The worst thing you can do is to do what he wants, do it poorly, and complain about how stupid it is to anyone even remotely willing to listen.

Make it easy for your boss to say yes. If you want your boss to approve, purchase, or do something, ask for it in a way that makes it easy for him to say yes. The key is in the preparation, in getting your facts straight before you ask. Think about what you're asking for. What will it cost? What are the risks? What are the benefits? Are there any alternatives? Do you have any suggestions on how best to do it? You want to bring your boss an idea he can work with, not one he has to work on. The more you have already done, the less he has to do; and the less he has to do, the easier it is for him to say yes.

Don't become your boss's friend. Be friendly, of course, but don't be friends. Your co-workers will resent you for it, and after a while, so will your boss. You see, when you and your boss are friends, it puts him into a no win situation—he can either be unfair to you so he can prove to your co-workers that he's not showing favoritism, or he can be unfair to them by showing you that favoritism. It's an uncomfortable position to be in, and some day, he might decide to get out of it at your expense. If you want friends, look somewhere else.

Mike Jacobs

Don't let your boss's incompetence be an excuse for your own. I know you're going to find this hard to believe, but some bosses are incompetent. For reasons we discussed earlier, they still become bosses. Bosses who don't know what they're doing can make it difficult for you to do your job, but only if you let them. So what if your boss is incompetent? You still have a job to do, and you have to do it well. If you screw up, your evaluation is not going to read, "He screwed up, but it's okay because his boss is incompetent." If you're going to succeed or fail, it's not going to be because of your boss, it's going to be because of the choices you make and the actions you take.

Never underestimate the power of an incompetent boss. He may be incompetent, but he can still hurt you; he can still make your life miserable at work, and fire you if he so chooses. There must be some reason that he's still the boss, and that may be reason enough for you to be watching what you say and/or do. Keep in mind, also, that he has the power, and you don't, and that he's going to do what he has to do to hold on to it. Just be careful.

Don't be a nuisance. There are some things that just seem to bother most bosses. If you know what's good for you, you won't "go there." So you have a good idea about where "there" is, I'll share with you some of their more common dislikes:

- They don't like to be "tested" to see how much they'll put up with. Employees like to do this so they can find a comfort zone, especially with a new boss. It makes bosses uncomfortable.
- They don't like to be told what your previous boss would have done.

132

- They don't like to be dragged into petty disagreements that cannot be resolved to everyone's satisfaction.
- They don't like to be told something "in confidence" that cannot be kept in confidence if something needs to be done about it.
- They don't like to be the last to know what they should be the first to know.
- They don't like it when employees go over their head without their knowledge.
- They don't like to do an employee's work when the employee can be doing it himself.
- They don't like to repeat themselves. They don't like to repeat themselves.
- They don't like to be made the butt of practical jokes, even if they have a good sense of humor.
- They don't like to listen to stupid, empty complaints.
- They don't like to deal with the same problem over and over.
- They don't like workers who are always doing things that they don't like having done.

If they don't like it, don't do it. Why press your luck?

SUMMARY

- Every job has an effect on every other job, before it and after it.
- A team is a group of people brought together to achieve a common goal.
- The key to getting along on a team is to get along with all of its members.

- We need each other and must work together. It is best, therefore, to look for the good in people and situations.
- A good boss can do a lot for you; a bad boss can do a lot to you.

Assignments:

1. At work over the next few days, go hunting for "jerk sightings," those moments when someone is acting like a jerk. DO NOT SHOOT THEM. Instead, take a mental picture of the moment and think about how foolish that person looked. Ask yourself if you want to look like that.

Lesson Ten:
Serving Your Employer

Objectives:

1. To recognize when you're being selfish with your employer.
2. To understand your employer's mission.
3. To appreciate the connection between effort, improvement, and results.

Talk about being selfish, if you go to work every day with the attitude that you're just going to put in your eight hours, do as little work as you can, and go home as soon as your eight hours are done, (so you can make it home on time to watch your favorite program), then you're being about as selfish as you can be. You're being a "warm body," and nothing more. Here's the problem with this—warm bodies are good for keeping warm, not for working.

Your employer has made a big investment in you. It recruited you, hired you, trained you, supplied you, and, of course, paid you, all so that you could help it to achieve its objectives.

These objectives, often presented as a mission statement, are generally broad in scope—to make a profit, to give investors a fair return on their investments, to be the employer of choice, to serve millions and millions, to serve and protect, to make a difference, to try harder, to provide quality as job one, to be the industry leader, to enrich the community, to grow, to please all customers, to give customers what they want, to provide service with a smile, to be number one...

These represent, for the business, the very reason for it to be in business, and the reason, too, for you to be on the payroll. If you want to remain on the payroll, and make more money, you need to buy into your employer's objectives. The more you buy in, the better off you'll be. Make it your objective to help achieve the company's objectives.

If you're going to do this, you have to understand that there's no room here for you to be selfish, no reason for you to be—

- Working overtime only when it suits your needs.
- Calling in sick when you're perfectly healthy.
- Staying home longer than you need to after an on the job injury.
- Stealing or destroying company property.
- Wasting time while you're on the clock.
- Doing things poorly just because you don't like doing them.
- Resisting change because you like things the way they are now.

Anything you do that makes more work for your co-workers, costs more money for your employer, wastes more time, creates more problems, causes more hard feelings, and otherwise makes life at work more difficult for everyone else, just so life can be easier for you, would be self serving. You cannot be self serving and serve your employer at the same time. These opposites truly don't attract.

Let's talk some more about this idea of "buying in" to your employer's objectives. First of all, you have to know what the objectives are. I'd be willing to bet, however, that most workers don't have a clue that their employer even has objectives, let alone what those objectives are. It's not like objectives are that hard to find. If they're not mounted on a wall, listed in the company's annual report, or included in your employee handbook, then all you have to do is ask.

Once you know what the objectives are, you can decide if helping to achieve them would be something you could feel good about, and something that wouldn't force you to compromise on your principles. If you're okay with them, you can buy in to them. The more you buy in, the better you feel; the better you feel, the better you do; the better you do, the more you help to achieve the company's objectives; and the more you help to achieve the company's objectives, the greater your rewards will be.

But, if you can't buy in, you might want to think about finding another job. Working for a company whose objectives you disagree with is not a healthy working relationship. So, if you think that serving millions and millions is too much, or that providing quality is, at best, job two, or that customers shouldn't have it their way, then you shouldn't be working for these companies. You should, instead, be working for a company whose mission is something like, "to serve only a few of whatever we want to serve without any regard for quality or customer satisfaction." That should be a fun job.

Results rule

If broad objectives are to be achieved, specific results must first be attained. Results will be the ultimate measure of your success. The hours you put

Mike Jacobs

in, the effort you put in during those hours, and the improvement that you show, will all be used to measure your success, but all three, together, are not as important as the results you get out. In the workplace, results rule.

All businesses, by the way, want basically the same results:

- More customers.
- More investors.
- Improved customer satisfaction.
- More sales.
- Fewer complaints.
- Fewer lawsuits.
- Fewer lost workdays from on the job injuries.
- Greater market share.
- Greater name recognition.
- Continued growth.
- Higher employee morale.
- Lower employee turnover.
- Less absenteeism.
- Less tardiness.
- Better public image.
- Increased productivity.
- Greater revenues.
- Lower costs.
- Higher profit margins.
- Bigger bonuses for upper management.

This is not just about for-profit businesses, either. Non-profit organizations and government agencies want these things, too, including lower costs and higher revenues. Being non-profit doesn't mean they're in business to lose money. They need money to keep operating.

Being dependent solely on philanthropic donations or government funding is not a safe thing for them to be, given the ups and downs of politics and the economy. They need to raise funds themselves, and be very careful with the funds they have. Actually, they make profits, too, but they don't call them profits, they call them retained earnings. It's the same thing.

It doesn't matter where you work; you're going to be judged according to the results you get. When you're getting good results, to your boss, no matter what else you do, you can do no wrong. Your results will speak for themselves.

If you're not getting results, no matter what else you do, it will not be good enough. You can be a loyal, dedicated, hard working, well dressed, good looking, highly intelligent, reliable, and enthusiastic employee, and a wonderful person, too, but if you're not getting results, you're still, in your boss's eyes, an underachiever, and your job is still going to be on the line. As Dr. Kelley observed, "highly committed and motivated incompetence is still incompetence."

Now, don't start panicking. There's still a place for some underachievers at work. Usually, it's working under the achievers. And there's still something to be said for putting in lots of hours, making a real effort, and showing improvement.

Putting in the hours is good, obviously, because it allows you the opportunity to do more, to put in a greater effort. But, it's only an opportunity. You have to do something with it, unlike many workers, who put in the hours, but little else. They show up at work, but not necessarily to work. What good is that?

Making the effort is good, too. It's through effort that results are achieved. The thing about effort, though, is that it doesn't always lead to results. Some people, try as they may, just can't get good results. Most bosses will appreciate their effort, but only for so long. If they see no improvement and no results, at some point they'll have to do something about it. They invest a lot of time and money into their employees, and sooner or later, they'll want to see a return on that investment, and you really can't blame them for wanting that.

Now, sometimes, if goals and objectives are set too low, results can be achieved with little or no effort. Achieving these results will not count for much because your boss will have expected them, and nothing less.

Showing improvement is always a good thing. Your boss will be very happy to see it. But as long as you're falling short of the results they want, you'll need to improve more. "Needs improvement," is not something you want to see on your performance evaluation. "Meeting or exceeding expectations," is so much better.

Here's what I recommend—put in the hours, make the effort, and show the improvement, but, make sure you put in enough hours, put as much effort as you can into those hours, and make the necessary improvements to ensure that you get the results your boss wants.

We have seen in this lesson the importance of putting the company's interests before your own, and we already know that by doing this, your own interests will ultimately be served. In lesson two, we learned that your job serves a purpose. Whatever its purpose is, it serves an even greater purpose—to achieve the results and objectives that the company is striving for. Your job was created for the express purpose of doing this. Your job is not at odds with what the company wants; are you?

SUMMARY

- Your objectives should be to help your employer to achieve its objectives.
- The effort you put in is more important than the hours you put in, but not as important as the results you get from your efforts.
- Employees are evaluated by the hours they work, the effort they put forth, the improvement they show, and above all, the results they achieve.

Assignments:

1. Ask your boss to tell you what the company's objectives are, and what, specifically, you can do to help achieve those objectives.
2. Ask yourself whether or not you can buy in to the company's objectives.

Lesson Eleven: Managing the Resources Available to You

Objectives:

1. To introduce the four resources that are available to you.
2. To learn how to manage these resources.

In this brief, but important, lesson, you will be introduced to the four resources you can make use of to better perform your job. A more detailed discussion will follow in lessons twelve through sixteen.

The resources are:

- Money (and the materials it can purchase)
- Time
- Information
- People

In lesson twelve, you'll learn how to manage money; in lesson thirteen, how to manage time; and in lessons fourteen and fifteen, how to manage information. Lesson fourteen will focus on information that comes in to you, while lesson fifteen focuses on information you send out, or communicate to others. Lesson sixteen will focus on managing people.

Actually, there is one more resource available to you. It's that magnificent looking person you see when you look in the mirror. Yes, you are a resource, too. Your knowledge, your skills, your energy, your enthusiasm, your passion...are all available to you, but as with any resource, must be used effectively.

Being resourceful

Managing resources effectively means being resourceful—getting what you need and using what you get, getting the most out of what you have and wasting as little as you can. You'll need to be resourceful when you consider that these resources are limited—there's a lot of money circulating about, but only so much available to you; there's all kinds of time available, but only so many hours in a workday; there's a glut of information out there, but only so much of any use to you; and there's millions of workers available, but only so many your employer can hire. They're even more limited when you realize that there are so many other workers and other businesses out there that are competing for the very same resources.

So, what must you do to be resourceful?

You find out what resources are available—how much money you have to spend, what supplies you have to use, how much time you have to work with, what information you can use, and which people can be of assistance. You can't use what you don't know is there to be used.

You get what you can of it by seeking it out and asking for it. Not by demanding it, not by expecting it, but by asking for it. If you don't ask for these things, you may not get them. Remember, there are lots of other people who are looking for them too.

You appreciate what you get. Knowing how important these resources are, and how limited too, you must be thankful that you have them and careful not to waste them. You must be careful that you use these resources and not abuse their use.

You use only what you need, no more and no less. For many workers, this is harder than it sounds. They'll use everything they can, even if they don't need to. This phenomenon is described by what has been called, "the law of availability," which tells us that if a resource, such as money, supplies, or time, is made available for use, it will be used, completely, even if it's not needed.

People can't help themselves, living in a world with such great abundance everywhere. With so much there for the taking, they take so much. They spend money they don't have, to buy things they don't need, to impress people they don't know, and then never use what they bought because they never really needed it. Sound familiar?

Use only what you need, please, and leave something for another time or for somebody else.

You make do with less. More is not always better than less. Having more of some things can make you wasteful; having less can help you to appreciate what you have, and be more creative or economical in using it. Too much money can lead to wasteful spending; too much time on your hands can lead to boredom; too much information can lead to confusion; too many people can lead to conflict, duplication of efforts, and even lower productivity.

"The law of diminishing returns" explains that too many workers can mean that less work will get done. That may sound odd, but it really isn't. What happens is that with more workers, more work will get done at first; as time goes by, however, each worker begins to do less. This is because of the conflicts and the duplication, but also because of the tendency of workers to slack off when they think that someone else will be there to pick up the slack. Once this starts happening, the group, as a whole, starts to do less.

So, when you're thinking about how much of a resource you should use, think "more or less."—before you use more, try to make do with less. The less money you use, the more will be left to buy other things; the less time you use, the more will be left to do other things; the less information you use, the better you will understand and the more you will remember. If you try to make do with less, but can't, then you can use more. You'll never know if you can make do with less unless you try.

You can use your resources wisely. Use it to do the things you should be doing, like serving your purpose and helping the company to meet its objectives. Don't throw your money or your time away on things that serve no one and help no one; don't gather information that you don't need to have; and don't ask your co-workers for help if you don't really need it or if they don't really have the time to do it. With supplies and equipment, read the instructions and do what they tell you to do. Use those as they were intended to be used.

You can be careful not to waste them. Wasting resources is not wise. They're limited, remember? There are others who would like to have them, remember? If you have money to spend, spend it on something you really need; if you have time, use it doing something productive; if you have information, do something with it; if you have co-workers willing to help, use them only when you really need them.

You can keep track of it. Keep a record of how much money you have and of how you spend it; keep a list of what you have to do, and a record of how you spend your time; sort and file the information you collect; and make a list of the people you meet with their contact information. Do this because you cannot manage anything unless you can see that it's being managed.

SUMMARY

- Money, time, information, and people, are limited resources that are available for you to use.
- Because they are limited resources, they must be managed carefully.

Assignments:

1. Read lessons twelve through sixteen, and do the assignments from those lessons.

Lesson Twelve:
Managing Money

<u>Objectives:</u>

1. To appreciate the value of money at work.
2. To develop a cost consciousness.
3. To learn how you can help your employer to make and/or save more money, and in doing so, to make more for yourself.

Most people don't give a damn whether
the company they work for is successful;
they care only that it be successful enough
to let them get what they want out of it.
—R. Hockheiser

Well, they should give a damn, and so should you. First of all, the company has made a huge investment in you in both money and time, and that alone, gives them the right to expect some return on their investment. If that return isn't sufficient, then there's no longer a reason for them to invest any more in you, is there? If you and your co-workers don't really care about the company's success, why should the company care about your job?

But here's the most important reason why you should give a damn—if you don't, you'll be missing out on a huge opportunity to make more money for yourself. You see, when you work for somebody else, the best way to make more money for yourself is to make more money for the company that you're working for. They'll be in a better position to pay you more, and you'll be in a better position to deserve more. "Helping others make money," writes Deepak Chopra, "and helping other people to fulfill their desires is a sure way to ensure you'll make more money for yourself as well as more easily fulfill your own dreams."

As a matter of fact

We're going to take a look at how you can help the company to make more money, and then, how you can help it to save more of the money it makes. But first, I think you need to get your facts straight about money and what it means to business. Knowing the truth about it will help you to understand why you need to do the things we're going to suggest that you do.

Fact #1—Money is a limited resource, which you already know. Contrary to popular belief, the government can't just print more of it whenever it feels like doing it, and the company you work for does not have all the money it could ever want or ever need, which means that there's no excuse for any worker to take something, break something, or waste something that belongs to the company, and then justify it by saying, "Well, they can afford it." They can't always afford it. If they could, if they had all the money they could ever want, they wouldn't need to be in business, would they?

Fact #2—Money is not the root of all evil, at least not in the workplace. It would be more appropriate to say that it's the root of all business. That's true, as we know, whether it's a for-profit business, a non-profit organization, or a government agency. They all need money. Without it, there would be no businesses, organizations, or agencies.

Only a small portion of the money a company makes will end up as profit. Not all revenue is lining some bigwig's pockets. The greater portion of it goes to paying bills, paying workers, paying taxes, providing services, making products, developing new and improved products, hiring more employees, expanding services and markets, and attracting new investors, who, by the way, are not too keen on investing in companies that are losing money. Whatever is left over is profit, which serves as the company's incentive to stay in business. As I see it, there's absolutely nothing evil about any of this, but if you see something different, let me know.

When all is said and done, it's all about money. Everything that happens at work, every action and every transaction, can directly or indirectly cost something or be worth something, and can be broken down into dollars and cents. In business, there's no such thing as something for nothing.

Fact #3—The "bottom line" is the bottom line. Revenues come in, expenses go out, and whatever remains is profit (before taxes, of course.) All three are important to a business, but profit is the most important thing. If you want to increase profits, there's only four ways to do it—increase revenues, decrease costs, increase revenues and decrease costs, and play with the books. I highly recommend you don't play with the books. It's not a game you want to risk losing.

Increasing revenues can be more fun, but according to some "experts," decreasing expenses can have a bigger impact on the bottom line. Not being one of those experts, I wouldn't know if that is true, but I don't

Mike Jacobs

really care, either. As far as I'm concerned, you should focus on both.

Fact #4—Some costs are necessary, and some costs are not. Sometimes, it seems like the company is only interested in cutting costs. It's like you're working for Mr. Scrooge. That's not the way it is. Businesses need to spend money to stay in business and to make even more money. They know they have to do this, and they're more than willing to do so, if the money is well spent. What bothers them is when they spend more than they have to, more than they can afford to, or any amount that could have been better spent on something else.

Any good businessman knows that it's just as bad to not spend money that should be spent as it is to spend money that should not be spent. When they don't spend what they should, needs go unmet and opportunities are lost; when they spend what they shouldn't, budgets go unmet and money is lost.

The simple truth is that some costs are necessary and some costs are not. Your job is to recognize the difference, and spend what you have to but save what you can. Waste of any kind is anything but necessary.

Fact #5—Costs do not control themselves. People control costs. If they don't, costs that are not controlled will almost always escalate out of control. For the company, it is so much easier to keep costs under control than it is to get them back under control; for you, it is so much more comfortable to be accustomed to controls than to adapt to new and tighter controls.

Fact #6—Workers are, at one and the same time, a business's greatest source of revenue and its greatest expense. Ironically, when businesses need to control their expenses, their only hope of doing so is with help from their workers, who are not always eager to help

150

even though it would be in their best interest to do so. Thinking about it, asking workers to help the company to save money can be like asking criminals to help solve their crimes.

Making money for the company

This is the easy part. It's simply a matter of taking what you've learned from the lessons and putting it to good use:

- Serving your purpose.
- Satisfying your customers.
- Spending your time productively.
- Getting results.
- Going the extra mile.
- Helping your co-workers.

Businesses that succeed, that are the industry leaders, are the ones that provide quality products and services, that are smart enough to draw customers in and good enough to keep them coming back. Workers who succeed are the ones who help the business to do just that. In my humble opinion, there is no room for providing anything less than the best you can give.

Saving money for the company

No matter how much money a company makes, it won't mean much if it spends even more. Then, there would be no profits and no incentive to stay in business. So, expenses must be kept in line, and to do this, the lines must first be drawn. That's what a budget is for. A budget is management's projection of what revenues and expenses will be for a period of time, usually one year. The expenses represent their idea of what the necessary costs of doing business should be. Their expectation will be that all expenses incurred during the year are necessary and within budget.

A funny thing happens, though, on the way to the bottom line—management doesn't always get what it expects. This is no real surprise when you consider that budgets are not always written using good business sense. Many are based, all or in part, on best guesses, wishful thinking, political maneuvering, sandbagging, showboating, and the arbitrary whims of upper management. Many are written to impress investors with projections that may look good, but are unrealistic.

Not that it will matter to you. You will be held to the budget no matter how unrealistic it is. When the lines have been drawn, you will be expected to stay within those lines even if the lines are in the wrong place and even if you don't know where the lines have been drawn.

How many workers ever get to see a budget? Not many, but they'll be expected to be in budget anyway. And when they go over budget, which is going to happen, especially when they don't know what the budget is, they're going to be called to task. Will claiming ignorance help? Of course not. Even if the budget's unreasonable, management is not going to admit it. They'll be more likely to point out that workers did a bad job than to admit that they wrote a bad budget.

Is this fair? No. Will it happen? Yes. Is there anything you can do about it? Yes, there is. You can ask to see the budget, at least as it applies to you and your department, and after you've learned where those lines are drawn, you can do your best to stay within them.

Before you spend any of the company's money, you can look to see if it's in the budget.

Of course, that doesn't always work because budgets have often been described as the last place to look for money. Why? Because every time you look for money, according to your boss, "it's not in the budget."

NEWSFLASH: It is in the budget! There's always money to be spent in the budget. Any boss who tells you otherwise is just using that as an excuse not to spend money. Any such boss is unfamiliar with the true purpose of a budget—to serve as a guideline, not a restriction. A smart boss will consider whether or not a cost is necessary, not whether or not it's in the budget. Unfortunately, they're not all smart.

Before we move on from this discussion of budgets, I want to share with you a little secret, which is especially good to know if you run a department, but good to know also if you don't run one. The secret is that the bigger and better budgets don't usually go to the departments that need it the most, but to the departments that either make the best case for it (they know how to ask), or demonstrate the best use of it (they know how to use it wisely.) It rarely goes to the department that only knows how to waste it. Think about it, who would you give your money to?

Alright, now that we've gotten that out of the way, let's talk about how you can save the company money by controlling costs. I have some good suggestions for you:

When your boss asks you to cut some cost, do your best to make it work. Do this, even if you think it's a mistake and even if you don't like doing it. Don't stand around, like so many workers do, complaining about how your boss is either cheap, greedy, or out of his mind, and don't do it halfheartedly so you can prove that your boss was wrong all along.

Mike Jacobs

NEWSFLASH: Cuts are going to be made. Budgets will be cut; hours will be cut; positions will be cut; and supplies will be cut. So unless you want to be one of the cuts that are made, get serious about making these other cuts work.

Make your own cuts. If you don't like it when your boss tells you that something has to be cut, then why don't you just make some on your own? Nobody knows your job better than you do, so who better to come up with ways to cut costs and save money? I'll tell you something, when you do this, you'll find it so much easier to work with ideas that are your own.

Do many workers do this? Of course not. They're too busy complaining about what the boss wants to take the time to think about things like that.

Sweat the small stuff. Ben Franklin said, "Beware of little expenses. A small leak will sink a big ship." Little amounts, added together, become big amounts, and add up quicker than you might think. When everyone is wasting just a little, taking just a little, losing just a little, and breaking just a little, before anyone knows it, there's just a little left. Bosses who appear to be cheap or greedy know this very well. They're not being cheap, mind you, they're being smart.

So pay attention to the little things—shut doors and windows when the air conditioning is on; turn off the lights when a room is not being used; use old memos for scratch pads; use the right sized paper for making copies; stop using the copier to make copies of your rear end; shut off faucets that are running; drink six cups of coffee instead of seven; stop using paper clips to pick your teeth; punch in and out on time...

Consider the costs and benefits of everything you do, without getting obsessive about it. Remember, in business, there is no such thing as something for nothing. Every purchase, every decision, every change, every action, and every reaction, has a cost, whether that be in dollars spent, time spent, energy expended, materials used, or manpower worked. Ultimately, all costs can be measured in terms of dollars and cents. Even when you can't pin a number on what something costs, there is always a number involved. There is always a cost that should be considered.

Then there are benefits, and although everything does have a cost, every cost does not have an equivalent or greater benefit. Now, if the benefit does not outweigh the cost, what you have is an unnecessary cost, and so, the potential benefits must also be considered. Costs and benefits, both, must be considered before you do anything.

In "higher circles," they call this cost/benefit analysis, but its use cannot, and should not, be limited to higher circles. All workers should be using it, and it's not that hard to do. It's simply a matter of asking, before you spend money, "Is it worth it?" But you have to ask!

Watch for hidden costs. Let's say that you're responsible for making purchases at work. How do you know if you're getting your money's worth, by its price? Not really. The cost of any item, you see, only begins with its price. There are always more costs involved, some of which may be hidden—taxes, shipping and handling, installation, training, breakage, and at least a dozen more. A good price, therefore, may not be good enough.

The relationship between price, quality, and service comes into play here. All things being equal, the lowest price is the best price. However, all things are rarely equal. You may have a combination of good service

Mike Jacobs

and high quality that would justify a higher price; or you may not have either, and that would negate a lower price. It all depends.

The highest or best quality may not even be the right quality for you. That also depends. If it's all that you can afford, and it gets the job done, its right for you, whether it's the best quality or not. The point I'm making is that you have to take everything into consideration before you make a commitment to purchase.

Use equipment and supplies as they were intended to be used. Even if you're not responsible for making purchases, you'll be held responsible for using them wisely. Good purchases can become bad purchases when things are not used properly. It's something that happens all the time, and it costs businesses billions of dollars every year.

Use only what you need. Waste not, want not. Don't get in the habit of using things only because they're available to be used. You can make do with less most of the time.

Stop wasting time. Time is money to your boss because you're on the time clock, and getting paid for all the time you spend at work. The waste of time is, arguably, the biggest waste of all, and because of its importance, lesson thirteen will be devoted entirely to it. So let's move on.

Be safe. Safety saves lives, limbs, and money. The costs associated with on the job injuries are staggering, running into the billions every year.

DID YOU KNOW? For every one dollar that your employer spends on worker's compensation, another ten dollars is spent on property damage, sick leave, medical expenses, overtime, training, re-training, reports, and employee counseling. The initial costs are only the tip of the iceberg.

DID YOU KNOW? For every one severe accident that occurs, there are ten minor accidents, thirty incidents of property damage, and six hundred near misses.

It seems that many workers are like accidents waiting to happen, and obviously, lots of accidents are happening.

DID YOU KNOW? According to the Chicago Tribune, there were 43,291 workers killed on the job between 1992 and 1998, compared to 47,393 American soldiers killed in Vietnam. How many more were injured? A great many more.

If you don't want to become a statistic, then practice good safety habits at work. Don't rely on the company's safety committee to protect you; protect yourself and your co-workers too—

- Stay home if you're too sick, tired, or hung over to stay alert.
- Report and/or remove any safety hazards you come across.
- Slow down.
- Refrain from horseplay.
- Get help when you need it.
- Help others when they need it.
- Follow directions and use equipment as it was meant to be used.
- Lift things properly, with knees bent and back straight.

Mike Jacobs

- Put things back where you got them from.
- Don't stack items too high.
- Use a ladder to reach high places.
- Close drawers when you're not using them.
- Make sure lighting is adequate.
- Don't leave wires exposed.
- Stay clear of co-workers who are acting strange (or stranger than usual.)

Listen, if you get hurt on the job, you're costing the company for what you're doing (collecting worker's comp) and for what you're not doing (working.) It's like double jeopardy, and it could jeopardize your job.

Don't steal from the company or destroy its property. (Or your co-workers' property either.)

DID YOU KNOW? Studies have shown that as many as 30% to 40% of workers have stolen something from their employers, and that another 30% to 40% admitted that given the right opportunity, they would steal from the company. By the way, these same studies have shown that bosses were the worst offenders because they have greater opportunities to steal and fewer people watching them.

A great many workers who get caught trying to steal try to justify their actions. The excuses they use are unbelievable. They're proof positive that people will say almost anything rather than admit that they did something wrong. For your amusement and amazement, I'll share some of these excuses with you:

- "I wanted to prove that I was smarter than my boss." (Obviously you're not, because you got caught.)

- "I'm entitled to it because they don't pay me enough." (How much is a thief worth nowadays?)
- "I needed it." (Why? Is it back to school shopping time again?)

Memo to Employees

With back to school shopping days upon us, we would like to make a request. We understand your desire to give your kids only the best, and we appreciate your dedication in not wanting to leave work to do your shopping, but we must ask that you do your shopping elsewhere, like in a store that sells back to schools supplies. Pencils, pens, paper, and paper clips were purchased by us for use by us. We know that you would never steal from us, but we ask that you not permanently borrow anything either. Management.

- "The company can afford it, and they even budget for it." (No, they can't afford it, and yes, they do budget for it, but as a precaution, not an invitation.)
- "It was just a little bit." (Yes, but if you'd steal just a little, what would you do if, given the opportunity, you could steal a lot?)
- "I figured it was there for the taking." (And how did you figure that? Was there a "take me" sign on it?)
- "I didn't think it was stealing." (Yes, we know, you were permanently borrowing it.)
- "Everybody else is doing it." (And that makes it okay because...?)
- "It was too tempting." (Why? Was it all wrapped up nicely with a big bow on top?)

Frankly, I don't believe people think of their office as a workplace anyway. I think they think of it as a stationery store with Danish. You want to get your pastry, your envelopes, your supplies, your toilet paper, six cups of coffee, and you go home.—Jerry Seinfeld

Stealing from the company is wrong, even if you don't really know that you're doing it.

DID YOU KNOW? Making personal phone calls at work, wasting time, using the copier for personal use, taking home pens and pencils, and padding your expense report are forms of stealing from the company, and no less costly and no less wrong than any other form of stealing.

Be an asset to the company, not a liability. Labor costs are the company's biggest costs. That includes you. Like other costs, you're in the budget. Like other costs, you must prove to be necessary to remain in the budget. You want to prove to your boss that you're an asset, not a liability, and that you're making the company more than you're costing it. The proof will be in your productivity.

When productivity improves, revenues will increase; when revenues increase, the pressures to cut costs are lessened. Then it's all easy.

SUMMARY

- When you work for someone else, the best way to make more money for yourself is to make more money for them.

- Money is at the root of all business.
- Some costs are necessary and some are not. The trick is to know the difference, and know enough to spend what is necessary and not spend what is not necessary.

Assignments:

1. Think about your job, and the tasks you do every day. See if you can come up with a way to do any of the tasks with fewer supplies, with fewer mistakes, with less help, with greater accuracy, in less time...Find a way to save the company money, put your idea in writing, and give it to your boss.

Lesson Thirteen: Managing Time

Objectives:

1. To learn how to use your time effectively.
2. To understand how time is wasted.
3. To understand the damage caused by wasting time.

Okay, I know you're going to think I'm crazy, but I want to start this lesson by telling you that you cannot manage time. How can you manage something that moves ahead at a steady pace regardless of any attempts to speed it up or slow it down? How can you manage something that once it has passed, can no longer be retrieved, except perhaps in your memory? How can you manage something that you can't see, hear, smell, or feel? How can you manage something that can heal all wounds, make people forget, reveal all truths, and make wine taste better, and has been around since the beginning of time?

We talk about time as though we can do so much with it, about how we can have time, waste time, save time, spend time, take time, make time, do time, lose time, make up time, and be on time, and how we can have time on our hands, time on our side, or time to kill. (If you kill time, will you do time?) And, of course, we talk about how we can manage time.

Look, I'm not trying to confuse you with all this rambling. I'm just trying to make a point, which is this—it's not about time, it's about you; it's about what you do in the time you have. It's not the amount of time you have that really matters, either; it's how you choose to use the time you have. If you choose to waste it, you'll never have enough of it.

Time, as a resource, is limited, not because time, itself, is limited, but because we, ourselves, are limited. We only have so much time on this earth, and we only spend so much of it at work. And, there's only so much time in a work day in which to get our work done.

So many workers foolishly waste the little time they have. As their work is left undone, they are often left, themselves, with this sick feeling, thinking, "I would've, I could've, I should've, but I didn't, and now it's too late."

The "paradox" of time

Time has been blamed for a lot of things that have not been done right or have not been done at all. "There wasn't enough time," has been one of the most frequently used excuses by workers everywhere. And that's all it is, an excuse.

"Everyone has all the time there is, but no one ever has enough." This is what's known as the paradox of time, and it raises a good question—how can you have it all, but not have enough? I would answer by saying that you only believe that you don't have enough. In truth, you do have enough if you choose to use wisely what you have. As Sheryl Crow sings, "It's not having what you want, it's wanting what you have." Wanting it and using it wisely.

Mike Jacobs

Think about this—you're doing something, and someone comes up to you and asks you to do something else. You don't really want to do it, so you say, "Sorry, I don't have the time." But you do have the time; you're just using it to do something else, something that you'd rather keep doing. Suppose someone else comes up to you, and asks you to do something that now interests you or is important to you. Would you tell that person that you didn't have the time? Maybe you would, but maybe you wouldn't. It's up to you to decide how you want to use the time that you do have.

Let me ask you this—have you ever wondered how two workers, given the same task and the same time to complete it in, could have such completely different outcomes? One could complete the task, with plenty of time to spare, and look for more to do, while the other could fail to complete the task, run out of time, and complain that there wasn't enough time to complete it in. The difference, you must understand, has nothing to do with how much time they had, but everything to do with how they chose to use it.

Are you starting to get the picture? Well, it's about time.

DID YOU KNOW? In a 2001 study by the Families and Work Institute, 28% of workers said they felt overworked most of the time, 28% said they felt overwhelmed most of the time, 59% said they felt one or the other some of the time, and 29% said they didn't have enough time to think about how overworked or overwhelmed they were.

Do you know why they're overworked and overwhelmed? Do you think it's because they have too much

164

work to do and not enough time to do it in? Or, do you understand now that it's because they don't know how to use their time wisely? I hope you understand.

I hope you also understand why it is so important that you use your time wisely, and not waste it foolishly. It's important because if you waste too much time, it hurts your employer and it hurts you just as much.

To your employer, time is like money, and depending on how it is used, it is either money made or money lost. When time is wasted, a great deal of money is lost.

Let's do a little arithmetic. Suppose a business employs 100 full time workers whose average wage is $22.93 an hour (our national average), and suppose that the workers, on the average wasted one hour a day, every workday for a year. The cost to the business over a year would be 100 (workers) X $22.93 (dollars) X 1 (hours wasted a day) X 260 (workdays a year) = $596,180.00, plus the cost of lost productivity. With 140,000,000 workers in the civilian workforce, can you imagine how much that would cost all businesses?

But wait! Do you honestly believe that workers waste only one hour a day? If so, you need some serious counseling. Businesses should only be so lucky. There have been studies done showing that workers waste 50% or more of their time at work. One study found that the average office worker spends only one and a half hours a day actually working. Now, I don't know who they studied or how accurate these studies were, and I imagine there must be other studies with different findings, but I do know that workers are wasting more than one hour a day.

DID YOU KNOW? In one study, 9% of workers admitted to spending up to one hour a day just surfing the Internet for personal pleasure. This alone was estimated to cost businesses $5.3 BILLION dollars a year. Frederick Lane, in his book, estimated the losses to be ten times that amount!

DID YOU KNOW? Many websites have an icon you can click on called the "boss is coming" icon, so when the boss is coming, you can click it and the screen will change to look like you're doing work. DID YOU ALSO KNOW that bosses aren't that stupid?

That's what it does to your employer. Unfortunately for employers, many workers couldn't care less about how much it costs the company as long as it doesn't come out of their own pockets. The way they see it, "the company can afford it," "it was just a few minutes," "everyone else is doing it," "I worked hard today so I deserve a break," and, "it's not like I'm stealing anything."

NEWSFLASH! They can't afford it; it's never just a few; everyone else is not doing it, and who cares if they are; you do get breaks; and it is stealing, because to employers, time is like money.

And by the way, it is coming out of the workers' pockets because when time is wasted:

- Workers are being less productive than they could be.
- They are putting undue pressure on themselves to meet deadlines.
- They are making more mistakes when trying to get caught up.
- They are forcing themselves to work more hours.

DID YOU KNOW? American workers are working longer hours than they did before and longer hours than their counterparts in other countries. On average, we're working 43 to 47 hours a week, which comes out to 350 more hours a year than workers in European countries. While this is due, in part, to increasing demands from employers, it is also due to our own inclination to waste time, forcing us to work even longer to make up for lost time.

If you haven't thought about this before, you need to start thinking about it now. When you waste time, you're hurting your employer and you're hurting yourself just as much. You can't keep doing this to yourself. It's not good for you. You need to make a decision now—to spend your time at work productively and not to waste your time at work needlessly. And just to set the record straight, there is always something productive you can do with your time...always.

One way or the other

There are three ways you can spend your time at work—

1. Being productive.
2. Being unproductive.
3. Being counterproductive.

Productive time is time spent doing anything that has, or adds value to the company—making sales, completing assigned tasks, collecting monies, cleaning the workplace, helping customers...Being productive is not to be confused with being busy. People can be very busy, or at least appear to be, but it doesn't necessarily mean that they're getting anything done.

Unproductive time, aka wasted time, is time spent doing anything that has, or adds no value to the company—socializing, grooming, gossiping, sleeping...

Counterproductive time is time spent doing anything that takes away value from the company—distracting co-workers, fighting with co-workers, destroying property, stealing...

During the course of your workday, you will spend your time one way or the other. At any given time, you can spend your time doing any one of the three, but you can't spend it doing all three. You have to choose, and you have to choose many times over throughout your day. If you know what's good for you, you'll choose more often to be productive, less often to be unproductive, and never to be counterproductive.

Notice that I didn't say you should never be unproductive. That's because it's okay to do some socializing, to have some fun, and to make sure that you're looking good. These things build camaraderie, strengthen the team, and make work more pleasurable. However, it can't be excessive; it can't take away too much of your productive time. Yes, you can socialize, have fun, and look good, but you're not there to do these things, you're there to work. These things can be done while you're doing your job, but not instead of doing your job. There's a big difference between the two.

Workers wasting time

Some workers are so good at wasting time, they can fall a month behind in their work in less than a week. They can be so creative in finding ways to waste time that it's almost inspiring, until you remember what they're doing. It makes one wonder how much they could accomplish if they only applied that creativity to being productive instead.

Why do workers waste so much time at work? There are many reasons, and it all depends on the person and on the moment:

- Some waste time because they don't know any better.
- Some because it just comes naturally to them.
- Some because that's what they were taught to do.
- Some because others are doing it.
- Some because nobody ever told them not to.
- Some because they think they have to.
- Some because they need to socialize.
- Some because they want to fit in.
- Some because they think they need a break.
- Some because they want to pace themselves.
- Some because they want to stretch tasks out.
- Some because they're trying to avoid doing something.
- Some because they feel they're not being paid enough to put in eight full hours.
- Some because it's only a few minutes here and a few minutes there.
- Some because they're mad at their boss.
- Some because it's fun.
- Some, just because.

Some day, some of these workers are going to get some sense and stop making some excuses for wasting some time. (That's some sentence.) There are no good excuses to waste any time. But waste it they do—

- By complaining to anyone and everyone who happens to come within the sound of their voice, but rarely complaining to anyone who could actually do anything about their complaint.
- By taking more time for breaks than they're entitled to.

DID YOU KNOW? Studies have shown that the average 15 minute break takes 23 minutes, and that the average 30 minute break takes 41 minutes. Some people never come back from breaks.

- By waiting to be told to do something when they already know that it has to be done.
- By clocking in late and clocking out early, and sometimes, even waiting by the time clock for several minutes until it's time to punch in or punch out.
- By gossiping about the boss, the new girl, a co-worker's marital problems, or anything else that has absolutely nothing to do with work.
- By spending too much time in the bathroom.

DID YOU KNOW? Studies have shown that workers do a lot more in bathrooms than just relieve themselves. It seems that bathrooms are good places to gossip as well as good places to discuss plans for lunch. (Gee, that must have been a fun study to participate in.)

- By grooming—combing their hair, putting on makeup, clipping their nails, picking their teeth, and checking themselves out in the mirror, all of which can easily be done at home, before they ever get to work.

- By socializing at the water cooler (thanks, apparently to HBO), the coffee pot, the copier, and, of course, the bathroom.
- By stretching tasks out to take longer than they should. Some workers can stare at the same page for so long, they get cross-eyed.
- By getting or sending personal phone calls or e-mails.
- By reading the paper, watching television, or listening to the radio, to keep up with the day's top stories, and then, sitting or standing around (again) talking about who won the big game, how the jury is going to decide, who's getting kicked off Survivor Island. Some of the bigger stories, like the O.J.Simpson trial, the Bill and Monica show, and the natural disasters of the recent past, have actually crippled businesses because so many workers were either staying home to follow them, or bringing their TV's with them to work.

I could literally go on for pages with examples of how workers waste time, but that would only be a waste of time. I just want you to realize that although there are many reasons why people waste time and many ways in which they waste it, there are more compelling reasons not to waste it, the most important being that time wasted is time not being productive.

The plain and simple truth is that workers may be putting in their eight or more hours a day, but they're certainly not working for eight or more hours a day, and that is working to their disadvantage.

Using your time productively

So, what do you do now? You already know that you need to spend less time being unproductive and no time at all being counterproductive. But how do you spend your time being productive?

1. You admit that you have a problem.
2. You save time by spending it.
3. You set priorities.
4. You get organized.
5. You make plans.
6. You start fast.
7. You take your time.
8. You use only the time you need.
9. You stop procrastinating.
10. You don't let everyone borrow your time.
11. You make things happen.
12. You simplify things.
13. You don't waste someone else's time.
14. You don't dwell on times past.

You admit that you have a problem. Wasting time is, to many of us, an addiction. If you happen to be among the many, I invite you to attend a brief meeting of TWA (Time Wasters Anonymous)—

"Welcome, you poor thing. Do not be ashamed, because you are among friends. All of us have suffered from the very same addiction as you. But we can help you to help yourself to overcome your addiction. All you need to do is follow our five step program.

1. Admit that you have a problem. (You know that you do.)

2. Stop finding reasons to waste time. (There are no good reasons.)
3. Start finding reasons not to waste time. (There are many.)
4. Stop wasting time. (Duh.)
5. Start being productive. (Double duh.)

Meeting adjourned. (We don't waste any time, do we?)"

You save time by spending it. Forget about saving time. Focus your attention, instead, on spending it. As long as you are spending your time doing something productive, there is little need to concern yourself about saving any of it. Of course, you can always do something more effectively or more efficiently, but that's really about spending time as well.

If you listen to the time management "experts," they'll tell you how you can save time. They recommend, for example, that to speed up meetings, you should make them "stand up" meetings and you should hold them right before lunch. The idea here is that the participants will be uncomfortable and hungry enough to move quickly through the meeting. It probably will work, but at what cost? What if the topic of discussion is important? Why would you want to move quickly through it and get nothing of any real consequence done? Look, if you need to discuss something important, hold a meeting, and make sure it's long enough and meaningful enough to get the job done; if it's not important, don't hold a meeting!

You set priorities. Have you ever heard of the 80/20 rule, otherwise known as the Pareto Principle? Well, it basically says that 20% of what you do accounts for 80% of what needs to get done. In other words, some things are far more important to be doing than others. What gets you results? What serves your purpose? Those are the things you need to do more of. I'll give you an example—in order to make sales, a good salesman will focus on making as many sales calls as he can make, knowing that, according to the law of averages, the more sales calls he makes, the more sales he will make.

Once you have determined what your priorities are, you need to spend whatever time you can working on them. Always remember that if something is important, it is worth doing, and if it is worth doing, it's worth doing right; if it's worth doing right, it's worth taking as much time as you need to get it done right. If it's not worth doing, it's not worth your time. Remember what we said about meaningless tasks—no matter how good you do them, they're still meaningless.

I know what you're thinking; there are things I have to do although they're not that important. Fine, save them up for when you have some time to spare, and do them all at one time. I guarantee, however, that as long as you're getting results and serving your purpose, no one's going to bother you about these things. That would be meaningless.

You get organized. "If I clean my desk, I'll never again experience the joy of finding something I had given up for lost." A co-worker of mine once told me that, and I still remember him well because he got fired when he lost a very important report that our boss needed. I remember, too, that the day he got fired was not a very joyful day for him.

It's not that difficult to get organized. It's just a matter of:

1.   Keeping your work area clean.

2. Filing things away neatly so you can find them quickly.
3. Making a list of things to do.

Another co-worker of mine complained that her "to do list" was getting too long. My advice to her was a) cross off anything that's been on the list for more than a week, because if nobody's bugging you about getting it done, it's obviously not a priority. You can always add it back later if you have to; and b) add two more things to your list—learn how to delegate and learn how to say "no."

One more piece of advice—don't overdo it. Spending time organizing and planning is good, but spending time producing is better. So, if your day planner is starting to weigh as much as you do, think about lightening up.

You make plans. Do you know why they say that failing to plan is like planning to fail? Because, when you fail to plan, you end up fighting fires, working someone else's agenda, and wasting lots of time. You're giving up control to whoever wants it and reacting to whatever happens. And so you fail.

You can make plans no matter what job you may have. If you're making deliveries, you can plan your routes; if you're holding a meeting, you can plan your agenda; if you're making a presentation, you can plan your speech; if you're doing many different tasks, you can plan your routine; and if you're trying for a promotion, you can plan your strategy.

You start fast. "The beginning," said Plato, "is the most important part of the work." As soon as you get in to work, start working. Once you get started, it will be much easier to keep it going. This we know from the "law of inertia" which teaches us that a body in motion tends to stay in motion.

If you start your day by wasting time, by fixing your hair, reading the newspaper, smoking a cigarette, drinking three cups of coffee, or sharing your life story with a co-worker, you will find yourself way behind schedule before you even get started. You will find yourself working, not on your priorities, but on whatever happens to come up, and as we both know, something's always coming up. The rest of your day will be spent playing catch up.

You take your time. "People will forget how fast you did a job, but they'll remember how well you did it," according to Howard Newton. (Unless, of course, you're running the 100 yard dash.)

In a hurry? What's your rush? If you're working on the things that you should be working on, there's really no need to rush. In fact, you'd be wise to slow it down so you don't risk making a bunch of stupid mistakes. If you make too many mistakes, it's going to take you even longer to finish because those mistakes will have to be corrected.

You use only the time you need. Parkinson's Law explains that work will either expand or contract in order to fill the time allotted for its completion. In simpler terms—whatever time you are given to complete a task, that is how much time it will take you to complete it. Let's say that your boss comes to you and tells you that he's giving you two hours to complete a task that normally has taken you only one hour to finish. The more you do it, the longer it will take you, until eventually, it will take you two hours. The reality is that it's not the job that takes longer to do, but you who takes longer to do it. That's because you're stretching it out to fill that extra hour.

Of course, it works the other way too—if it takes you two hours now, and you're asked to get it done in one, you'll eventually find a way to do it in one. Your boss, by the way, is well aware of this.

Most workers will stretch out tasks to fill their days, and if left with any time to spare, will find a reason to waste it. Smart workers, like yourself, will use only the time they need to do their work, and if left with time to spare, will look for opportunities to use it productively. You are smart, aren't you?

You stop procrastinating. Call me crazy again, but I must tell you that there are times when it pays to procrastinate. I can think of at least five good reasons to put off doing something:

1. When you don't know how to do something.
2. When you already have too much to do.
3. When there's something more important to do.
4. When you're too sick, tired, or distracted to do it right.
5. When you've already screwed up enough.

Sometimes, it's just better to postpone success than to move ahead and guarantee failure. Usually, though, it's better not to procrastinate. This is because the more you put off doing something, the harder it gets to do, and the less time you have to do it in. With less time, you're more likely to do it wrong, and since something is always coming up, some things, if put off, will never get done unless someone else does it. People are not always happy about doing for you what you should have done for yourself.

If something needs to be done, do it as soon as you can. If, however, it's something that isn't important, or something that someone else should be doing, then put

Mike Jacobs

it off...forever. I always say, why put off for tomorrow what you can put off forever?

You don't let everyone borrow your time. People are always looking to borrow your time—"Can you give me a hand?" "Have you got a minute?" "Are you busy right now?" "Could you do me a favor?" As long as you're willing to lend your time, there'll be no end to those looking to borrow it.

The next time someone asks you if you have a minute, ask him if it will only take a minute. It rarely does. Then, if you want, you can say yes, but at least you have some idea of what you're getting yourself into. Remember, you still have your own work to do, and you can't be lending time that you don't have to lend.

Now, if you don't "have the time" or don't want to lend the time you have, you can say no. As long as you're not being arbitrary (saying no "just because"), and you have a good reason to say no (such as having something more important to do), and you're being polite, most people will understand, and move on to find someone else with time to lend.

Ways to say no (and what you're really thinking)

"I wish I could help." (but I'm glad I can't)
"When I get around to it." (which I won't)
"I'll sleep on it." (but I won't lose any sleep over it)
"I'll get back to you soon." (as soon as you get someone else to do it)
"I wish you had asked me sooner." (although I still would have said no)
"I'm sure you can do it better yourself." (Not really, but I'd like it better that way)

You make things happen. It's been said that there are three kinds of people in this world—those who make things happen, those who watch what happens, and those who wonder what happened. We talked earlier about using your initiative, and that's what it's going to take to place yourself in that first group of people.

Rest assured, if you only wait to be told, you will waste a lot of time waiting. If you give up control of your time to other people, you will never be able to use it in your best interests.

You simplify things. Whatever you do, there is almost always a better way to do it, and you should be looking for that better way. You need to look at the various tasks you perform, and ask yourself if there's a way to do them more effectively, more efficiently, or more economically, or in a different way, a different order, a different time, a different place, with different tools, or with different people helping.

Nobody knows your job better than you. Nobody has a better right to ask these questions, a greater ability to answer them, or a greater need to find the answers. It's your job, and you should always be looking for ways to do it better, and never settling in to doing it a certain way because "that's the way you've always done it."

You don't waste someone else's time. Your co-workers' time is as important to them as your time is to you. So don't take your breaks where they're still working; don't complain to them about things they can't do anything about; don't dump your work on them; don't call in sick if you're not sick, leaving them to cover for you; and don't look to borrow their time if they don't have time to lend.

You don't dwell on times past. It's a waste of your time. You know you're going to make mistakes, do stupid things, make bad decisions, assume the wrong things, have misunderstandings, forget to do what you need to do, miss out on opportunities, and create a few hard feelings along the way. It's okay; people do these things all the time, and, in case you haven't noticed, life still goes on. So, why don't you go on about your life? Fix what you can, learn what you can, and remember what you will, but don't dwell any longer, beating yourself up over what's been done. What's done is done. Any time you spend dwelling on what's been done, will be time you cannot spend working on what still has to be done, and working towards the future.

Remember the past
Live in the present
Look to the future

Time is not something you can take for granted. Its here before you know it, and gone before you can do anything with it, and the cost of wasting it is too high a cost to pay. Realize that if you come to work late, leave early, take extra time on your breaks, and waste all kinds of time in between, you are stealing from your employer, putting an added burden on your co-workers, and cheating yourself out of valuable time you could be using to be more productive. Is that what you want? I hope not.

SUMMARY

- You cannot manage time, but you can manage what you do in the time you have.
- What matters is not the amount of time you have, but the way you choose to use that time.

- If you waste your time, you'll never have enough of it.
- Spend as much time as you can being productive, as little as you can being unproductive, and none being counterproductive.
- Remember the past, live in the present, and look to the future.

Assignments:

1. For one week, keep a log of how you spend your time. Next to each entry, put a P for productive, a U for unproductive, and a C for counterproductive. At the end of the week, total all the P's, U's, and C's. See how you fare. Think about the U's and C's and how you can eliminate them from your daily activities.

2. Clean up your work area. Get rid of anything that you haven't used for a long time and will probably never use again, anything that's covered in dust or spider webs, and anything that can be used against you in a court of law.

Lesson Fourteen:
Managing Information

<u>Objectives:</u>

1. To understand what good information is.
2. To learn how to find the best information.
3. To appreciate the importance of using the best information.

The trouble with the world is not that people know too little, but that they know so many things that ain't so.—Mark Twain

So many workers are clueless. They lack the information they need to be the best workers they can be. Surely, management is partially to blame for this by not always making this information available to its workers, but workers must also share the blame. When they don't ask for help when they need it, when they don't ask for clarification when they don't understand something, when they don't attend training programs, when they don't pay attention at training programs, when they don't follow directions or read instructions, when they don't listen, when they don't ask questions, and when they don't go looking for the best information, of course they're going to be clueless.

When these workers make assumptions, when they jump to conclusions, when they participate in gossip, when they listen to the wrong people, and when they believe everything people tell them to believe, how could they not be clueless? Yet they still have the nerve to say, "Nobody ever tells me anything around here." Give me a break. Everybody's trying to tell them something, but they're not listening!

Listen up, in today's workplace, all workers will need to be better informed. Their success will depend greatly on their ability to know what they're doing and to know what they're talking about before they do or say anything.

The information is out there to be had. In fact, there's far more information out there than you could ever possibly need. You could easily be overwhelmed by it all unless you know what you're doing.

What should you be doing? You should be actively seeking out the best information, sorting it out from the information you don't need, and putting it to good use, all of which you will learn to do in this lesson.

And what happens when you don't have the best information? You make bad decisions, are unable to solve problems, waste lots of time, make stupid mistakes, upset lots of people, hurt lots of feelings, create misunderstandings, say things you live to regret, and embarrass yourself in more ways than you can ever imagine. Being uninformed or misinformed is no way to be, not if you want to be happy and successful.

The best information

If you want to find something, it helps to know what you're looking for. What, then, is "the best information?" It is information that is—

- Accurate
- Relevant

- Timely
- Sufficient

It is accurate, being based on first hand observation and established facts, and not on hearsay, gossip, opinion, wishful thinking, feelings, or guesses.

It is relevant, having something to do with the task at hand, and not just some interesting little tidbit that has nothing to do with your job. When you have a need to know, things that are nice to know only get in your way.

It is timely, being current, up to date, and available when you need it, and not available only after it's already too late. Information is useless to you if you don't have it when you need it. It does you no good to say, "I wish I knew then what I know now."

It is sufficient, being just enough for you to use, not too little, which leaves you wanting for more, and not too much, which leaves you confused and overwhelmed.

Finding the best information

Seek and ye shall find. Now that you know what you're looking for, let's see how you can go about finding it. It's not difficult if you:

- Go looking for it.
- Stop looking when you have enough.
- Keep an open mind.
- Consider all sources.
- Don't believe everything you see or hear.
- Don't assume anything.
- Ask questions.
- Listen carefully.

Go looking for it. If you don't go looking for it, how would you ever know if it was accurate, relevant, timely, and sufficient? If you don't go looking for it, one or more of these five things will happen—

1. You may never get any information, because some people won't give you information unless you first ask them for it, and some people won't give it to you simply because they don't want you to have it.
2. You may get information, but it won't be what you need, because people will often tell you what they want you to hear, or what they think you want to hear, without really knowing what you need.
3. You may get information, but it will be too little to be of any use or too much to make any sense of.
4. You may get information, but it will come too late for you to use.
5. You may actually get the best information. But if I were you, I wouldn't hold my breath waiting for it. It's too important that you have the best information, and it can only be had by looking for it, and not by waiting, wishing, wanting, or hoping for it.

When you sit back and wait for information to come to you, you will get what you get, whether you like it or not, whether you need it or not, and you'll have no one to blame but yourself.

Stop looking when you have enough. There comes a time when enough is enough. There's so much information out there from which to choose. Everybody's either selling, telling, asking, suggesting, recommending, reporting, or hinting at something. Everyone, it seems, has an opinion on everything. At some point, you just have to say, "enough."

Many people suffer from what is called, "paralysis by analysis." They are so determined to be 100% sure of things, and so convinced that they have to wait until "the time is right," to do things, that they never get anything done. For them, there is never enough information. What you must realize is that you may never be 100% sure of anything and the time may never be exactly right. It doesn't matter, because you don't have to 100% sure of anything, and as long as the time isn't exactly wrong, you'll always be alright.

Keep an open mind. "My mind is made up," said Dave Farber, "don't confuse me with the facts." Many people look only for "facts" that fit with their opinions. Anything that doesn't fit will be overlooked or misinterpreted. This might be convenient if you're a lawyer defending someone who's guilty, but not if you're just trying to do your job. If you want to do it right, you have to keep an open mind. You have to accept information even if you don't like it, even if it hurts you, scares you, makes you mad, or makes you feel uncomfortable, and even if it doesn't fit with your opinions or your beliefs.

Yes, the truth sometimes hurts. Sometimes you really don't want to hear it, but, for your own good, you must. Criticism, as an example, can be hurtful. Nobody really wants to hear that they're not doing as good as they should be doing. But if you want to do better, you need to know how you're doing, whether that is good or bad. For you to believe that you're doing a good job when, in fact, you're not, is grossly unfair to you.

Consider all sources. An old Kenyan proverb tells us—"He who does not know one thing knows another." Everybody knows something, and everybody can teach you something, if not from what they know then from what they don't know. The best information usually comes from the best sources, but it can come from anyone and anywhere. Even a fool can sometimes be right, just as a genius, like myself, can sometimes be wrong, or so I've been told a number of times.

Of course, some sources are better than others. The best sources are usually people who are close to a situation ("in the know"), who rely on the information (have a "need to know"), who have a track record of being right, or who have no reason to lie. These are the sources you consider more often.

Less reliable sources are usually people who are far removed from a situation ("out of the loop"), who don't have to rely on the information (but want to know anyway), who are always looking to spread rumors or stir up trouble, who have lied before, or who have something to gain by lying. These are the sources you should consider less often.

Speaking of unreliable sources, you should always remember the first Law of Expert Advice—"Don't ask the barber if he thinks you need a haircut." What do you think he's going to say?

Some sources should be considered more and some should be considered less, but all should be considered some before you accept information and act on it. So, the next time someone tells you something, consider what he's saying, but consider it carefully. Ask yourself, "How reliable is this person?" "How would he know this information?" "Does he have anything to gain by telling me this?" Ask him some questions too, and accept the information only after you've considered it carefully.

Don't believe everything you see or hear. People will believe almost anything. If they overhear other people talking about something, they'll believe it; if something is whispered to them, they'll believe it, as if being a secret makes it true; if it's in writing, they'll believe it, as if being "right there in black and white" makes it true; if it's presented in the form of a statistic, they'll believe it, as if numbers didn't lie; if it's what they want to hear, or if it fits their opinions, they'll believe it, as if wanting it makes it so; if it's told to them by someone they think they can trust, they'll believe it; if it's the first thing they hear, or the last, they'll believe it, too. You can believe me when I tell you this.

The problem is that none of these things are good reasons to believe anything, including me telling you that you can believe me (although you can believe me.) The information may be good, but then again, it may not. In a great many cases, it's not. The point is that you need to clarify it so you understand it, and verify it so you know that it's true.

Let me tell you a few things about people, and the information they give you. Maybe this will help you to understand why it's so important that you clarify and verify information before you say or do anything based on that information—

- People tend to believe what they want to believe. They see things from their own unique perspective. "Beauty" is not the only thing "in the eyes of the beholder." So when they tell you something, it may be colored by what they believe.

- People, for some reason, like to be the bearers of either good or bad news. They want to be the first to give you the news, so in their haste, they may be less informed than they think they are.
- People will take what they hear, and put it into their own words. A lot will get lost in the translation.
- People have a tendency to generalize, making things seem bigger and broader than they really are. If they see two people doing something, it becomes, "everybody's doing it;" If they hear one person complain, it becomes, "Nobody's happy;" If something goes wrong, it becomes, "It's always something in this place;" If they don't get a memo, it becomes, "They never tell me anything around here." Rarely is it ever "everybody," "nobody," "always," or "never," except to them. (Note: when I tell you to always or never do something, I'm speaking in general terms about what's best for you. You don't have to do anything I say, but then, you'd never be happy or successful, would you?)
- People will exaggerate things by adding in some details of their own, or will simplify things by leaving some details out.
- People who want you to do something or buy something will tell you what they want you to know so you will do what they want you to do.
- People don't always say what they mean (they may be afraid of being rejected or of being wrong, or of offending you, hurting you, or being hurt by you); they don't always mean what they say (they may be lying to protect

themselves or to gain an advantage over you); and, they don't always know what they're saying (they may be misinformed, tired, or overly emotional), which, unfortunately, never stops them from talking.

People are people, what can I say? You have to listen to them, but you can listen carefully. So, the next time somebody tells you that "everybody's" doing something, ask what they mean by "everybody." I guarantee they'll quickly change their tune.

Don't assume anything. Given what we know about people, it would make no sense to assume anything. Life also teaches us that—

- People are capable of anything, both in and out of character.
- Nothing lasts forever.
- Things are not always what they seem to be.
- The past is no prediction of the future.
- There is nothing common about common sense.
- You can never underestimate the power of human stupidity.
- Times change.
- Wishing doesn't always make it so.
- When something can go wrong, it will go wrong.
- When something can't go wrong, it will still go wrong.
- The best laid plans of mice and men often go astray.
- You just never know.

Assumptions can be right, but they are more often wrong. That's because they're based on inaccurate and unreliable information. Making an assumption is like judging a behavior that you don't understand; your judgment is based on what you think you know, and not on what you really know.

We all make assumptions, and we all have regrets for doing so. Here are some of the most common assumptions we make:

- That because we explain something to someone, he understands it.
- That because we didn't notice something, it's not there.
- That because something is important to us, it's important to others.
- That because someone is saying nothing, he has nothing to say.
- That because nobody is complaining, everybody's happy.
- That because something has always been done, it should always be done.
- That because something is forbidden, it is bad.
- That because something is encouraged, it is good.
- That because "everyone's" doing something, we should be doing it too.
- That because someone is educated, he is smart.
- That because someone is "unedumicated," he is stupid.
- That because we do someone a favor, it will be appreciated.
- That because we told someone to do something, it will get done.

Mike Jacobs

- That because someone is doing a job poorly, he is unable to do any better.
- That because someone does something bad, he is a bad person.
- That because something should happen, it will happen.
- That because the boss doesn't use our ideas, they are bad ideas.
- That because someone is of a particular age, gender, race, or national origin, he or she is going to act in a certain way.

Can you see how making assumptions can get you into big trouble, how it can force you to make mistakes, waste so much of your time, hurt or anger so many people, create so much misunderstanding, and cause you so much embarrassment? Wouldn't it make so much more sense to just stop making assumptions? You would assume so.

Ask questions. Don't be afraid to ask if you need help, if you don't understand something, or if you're looking for the best information. Don't be afraid, either, of asking a stupid question. The people who look stupid are not the ones who ask stupid questions, but the ones who don't ask questions when they should be asking, and as a consequence, do stupid things. Are there stupid questions? Sure there are, but unless you're a contestant on "Jeopardy," it's not going to hurt you to ask.

The best reason I can think of for asking questions is that unless you ask, most people will not offer you the help, the explanation, or the information that you need. Sometimes, it's because they're assuming that since you're not asking, you don't need to know. However, most people, if you do ask, will gladly give you the answers you seek. It's like they feel obligated to answer. Of course, there are always some folks who are too selfish or guilty to answer any questions. In that case, you just ask someone else.

There's a way to ask for what you need. It involves being polite and non-threatening, and asking only because you are seeking clarification or verification. It does not involve being rude or offensive, annoying or challenging. You can't annoy people like a child asking "Why?" over and over again; you can't challenge people like a lawyer trying to get someone to incriminate himself; you can't badger someone like a reporter trying to get an exclusive story. You're asking because you need to know something; it's not an inquisition or an interrogation. So,

- If someone says "Everyone's upset," you ask, "Everyone?"
- If someone says, "You need to improve," you ask, "In what way?"
- If someone says, "Do it ASAP," you ask, "By when, and what about my other work?"
- If someone says, "Your attitude stinks," you ask, "What, specifically, did I do wrong?"
- If someone says, "Never do that again," you ask, "Never?" and "why not?"
- If someone says, "I think you're wrong," you ask, "What makes you think that?"

You don't ask things like, "Are you talking to me?" "Who asked you for your opinion?" "Do I look like I care what you think?" "Since when did you become my mother?" or, "Who died and left you in charge?"

The most successful workers are those who ask the right questions about what needs to be done, not

Mike Jacobs

the workers who only question why they have to do anything—

- Successful workers ask, "Why are we doing it like this?" and not, "Why do we have to do this?"
- Successful workers ask, "What if we did it this way?" and not, "What if we didn't do this?"
- Successful workers ask, "How can we do it better?" and not, "How can we get this done before five o'clock?"
- Successful workers ask, "Have we overlooked anything?" and not, "Haven't we done enough yet?"
- Successful workers ask, "What's the best use of my time right now?" and not, "What can we do to pass the time?"

Listen carefully. Kenneth Wells tells us that, "A good listener tries to understand thoroughly what the other person is saying. In the end he may disagree sharply, but before he disagrees, he wants to know exactly what it is he is disagreeing with."

God gave you two ears and one mouth for a reason—so you could do more listening and less talking. If you're looking for the best information, that's not a bad idea. You can't learn much by talking other than how much or how little you already know.

When you listen to people, you have to really listen. It's not enough that you hear sounds coming out of their mouths; you have to be able to identify what those sounds are. To do that, you must make eye contact, pay attention, be patient, and be responsive. I'll explain, so be patient with me, stop thinking about dinner, and pay attention.

Eye contact lets people know that you're listening, which they usually appreciate unless they just like to hear the sound of their own voices. It also allows you to observe their facial expressions and their body language as they speak. What people say and what they're doing when they say it, does not always match. That's when you need to start questioning what they're saying. If, for instance, someone is telling you that he's not mad, but he's gritting his teeth, clenching his fist, and turning beet red, it would be fairly safe to say that he's mad.

Paying attention, or focusing, helps you to better understand and remember what is said. People always appreciate having your undivided attention. The key to paying attention is to remove any and all distractions or to move the conversation to a less distracting place.

Patience, as we've been told, is a virtue. It can help you to pick up on information that you would otherwise miss. To be patient means to resist the urge to talk. If someone is talking too slow or is too difficult to understand, you can't just jump in and finish their thoughts for them. Nor should you jump to conclusions or make any assumptions about what they're trying to say. You cannot assume, either, that they use words the same way you use them. With age and cultural differences being what they are, words can mean different things to different people.

Being responsive helps to foster understanding. Every so often, as the other person is speaking, you either repeat or rephrase what they're saying to show that you're listening and ensure that you understand. You can say things like, "So what you're saying is...?" "I see," "I understand," "I know what you're saying," or how about, "I feel you, dude." You can also nod your head in agreement. (Or, you can disagree too.)

And that's how you can find the best information. And when you have that information, that's when you must have the good sense to use it. Unless you're working as a census taker, a researcher, or have some other such job, you're not getting paid just to be informed; you're getting paid to perform to the best of your ability, using the information you have. Have the good sense, also, to use the best information and the best ideas, regardless of who they came from. You will not always be the one with the best ideas, but you can always be the one who uses them.

SUMMARY

- All workers need to be well informed.
- You must go looking for the best information, and use it when you find it.
- The best information is accurate, relevant, timely, and sufficient.
- You are not getting paid to find information, but to use it.

Assignments:

1. Review the list of common assumptions we make. See if you make any of them, and if you do, stop making them.
2. Listen for generalizations that people make over the next few days, and ask them to explain.

Lesson Fifteen: Communicating

Objectives:

1. To understand the importance of communication in the workplace.
2. To appreciate the need for understanding.
3. To learn your role in helping to reach an understanding.
4. To learn how to be an effective communicator.

Comedian Chris Tucker's favorite line is, "Do you understand the words that are coming out of my mouth?" Unfortunately, in the workplace, we don't always understand each other. Many workers are unable to make themselves understood, and many others are unable to understand. Because of this, anything that can be misunderstood will be misunderstood.

If you are to be successful, you must be able to communicate back and forth with your co-workers, and share ideas with them. You must become an effective communicator. People must be willing to listen to you, be able to hear what you're saying, and be able to understand what you said.

If you want them to understand you, you cannot hope that they do or assume that they do, you must make sure that they do understand. That's your responsibility. Yes, understanding is the key to effective communication, but you are the key to understanding.

Chisholm's Third Law suggests that, "If you explain so clearly that nobody can misunderstand, somebody will." I wouldn't worry about that. Some people just don't understand anything, and in those cases, all you can do is shake your head and laugh it off. If you want to worry about something, worry about being understandable.

In lesson fourteen, we learned how to find the best information; in this lesson, we'll learn how to give the best information to others. It's important that you be one of those reliable sources that people will consider more often. It will not serve your best interests to be known as a "fountain of misinformation."

Being an effective communicator

What you have to say either comes out of your mouth, on a piece of paper, in an e-mail, or over the Internet. To be an effective communicator, you must know how to use all four. The suggestions that follow will apply, for the most part, to all four. The biggest difference is that with putting things in writing, in an e-mail, or on the Internet, you're establishing a permanent record for all to see. You're literally putting yourself out there, which makes it critical that you have a good working vocabulary and good writing skills. Mistakes in spelling, grammar, and style are quite noticeable when in writing, exposing your limitations for all to see. So, learn how to write, because at some time or another, you will need to put something in writing, be it a memo, a resume or application, a report, or even a letter of resignation.

You'll have to decide which means of transmission you will use. Should you meet with someone face to face so you can see how he reacts? Should you put something in writing so there's a permanent record of it, and so nobody can say that you never told them so?(although there'll always be someone who swears he never got the memo.) Or, should you do both?

It all depends on the situation—who you're talking to, how important it is, how urgent it is, and whether or not it's personal. I would suggest, however, that doing both has some definite advantages. You have to be careful, though, not to mix up your messages. You can't say one thing and put something else in writing.

To be an effective communicator, then, you need to—

- Know what you're talking about.
- Not pretend to be a "know it all."
- Know when to stop talking.
- Get to the point.
- Speak up.
- Speak the truth.
- Speak for yourself.
- Pay attention to what you're doing while you're talking.
- Remove all barriers to effective communication.
- Take responsibility for reaching an understanding.

Know what you're talking about. "Blessed is the man," wrote George Eliot, "who, having nothing to say, abstains from giving in words evidence of the fact." Hey, if you don't know what you're talking about, you shouldn't be talking, unless, of course, you want everybody to know that you don't know what you're talking about, or you like saying things that you'll later regret saying. Because that's what's going to happen if you keep talking.

Too many people talk without knowing what they're talking about. More often than not, they learn that it's much easier to let words out of their mouths than to take them back. They learn, too, that sticks and stones may break some bones but words can also hurt.

So, get your facts straight before you say anything. Before you criticize someone, be sure he deserves the criticism; before you praise someone, be sure he is worthy of that praise; before you ask someone to do something, be sure he's the right person to ask and it's the right thing to do; before you tell people how things should be, be sure you know how things should be; and, before you write a book like this, be sure of what you write.

Don't pretend to be a "know it all." As Robert Mueller put it, "Those who think they know it all are very annoying to those of us who do." Really, there's no need to show people how much you know or how many big words you can use. They don't really care, and all you're going to do is to insult them and make them angry. You're not going to impress anyone with your brilliance. If they're going to be impressed, it will be with how helpful your message is, and not with how brilliant you are. If you must show off how much you know, either become a contestant on a game show or buy a game of Scrabble.

Know when to stop talking. Obviously, a good time to shut up would be when you don't know what you're talking about, but there are other good times as well—when you've already said too much, when you're angry or in some other emotional state, when you have nothing nice to say about someone, when it appears that nobody's listening, and, above all, when someone else, especially a customer, is talking.

As Courtois's Rule states, "If people listened to themselves more often, they'd talk less." So if none of the reasons above are good enough reasons for you to stop talking, try listening to yourself.

Get to the point. The less said, the better. Not many people have total recall. Most of them can only remember a small portion of everything they see or hear. The more you say, the more it confuses them, and the less they remember. There's only so much information anyone can handle and only so much time in a day.

Keep it short and simple. (KISS, aka keep it simple, stupid.) Use words that people can understand, don't use generalizations, and don't use technical terms or abbreviations unless you explain what they mean. Homosapiens are easily perplexed when subjected to discombobulated configurations of verbose wordage, and that renders them choleric. (Okay, so I used a dictionary. Sue me.) In other, more understandable, words—people get confused when you use big, fancy words, and that makes them mad.

Speak up, or forever hold your peace. While you may regret some of the things you say, you are more likely to regret the things you don't say when you should have said them.

Speak up when you don't understand an instruction you've been given. It's better to ask, "What am I supposed to do?" than to ask, "What was I supposed to do?" People aren't mind readers, although some would like you to believe otherwise. They won't know that you don't understand unless you tell them that you don't.

Speak up if you disagree with something. It's okay to disagree as long as you're not being disagreeable.

Mike Jacobs

Most people will appreciate your honesty. If you don't speak up at first, you'll have no right to come back later and say, "I told you so."

Speak up if something or someone is bothering you. It does you no good to keep things that are bothering you pent up inside. It just makes you sick, gets you even madder, and allows the problem to continue. If you're mad at someone, don't badmouth him to the other workers; go to him, instead, and tell him how you feel. In all likelihood, whatever's bothering you will be bothering him too, and you'll both be glad that you talked it over.

What if it's your boss who's bothering you? What do you do then? You do the very same thing as you would do with anyone else. You speak up, but you remember not to speak out. Sam Goldwyn once said, "I want my people to speak up and be honest, even if it costs them their jobs." He was kidding, of course. Only an incompetent boss would fail to see the value of an employee who has the courage to speak up.

And speak up, as we said earlier, when you see things that shouldn't be happening, like safety hazards, theft or destruction of company property, violations of company policy, incidences of harassment or discrimination, and acts of violence. Never assume that someone else will speak up instead.

Speak the truth. It's easier to tell the truth than to tell a lie. The truth is the truth, no matter how many times you tell it. With a lie, you have to remember what you said and who you said it to, and the more times you tell it, the harder it gets to remember, and the easier it is to get caught.

Some would say that the truth can sometimes hurt. This may be true, but you have to think of it as being like a tooth extraction—it hurts when you're getting it done, but it always leads to a much better condition. Besides, it hurts a lot more to get caught in a lie, and that's the truth.

Speak for yourself. Don't be asking one person to tell another person what you should be telling him yourself. The longer it takes for information to get from you to someone else, and the more people it has to pass through, the more distorted it will be when it gets there. As your message gets retold in someone else's words, the message, itself, will almost never be the same. Unless you really don't care whether or not the right message is received, you should deliver it yourself.

Pay attention to what you're doing while you're talking. It's important that you sound like you know what you're talking about, and act like you mean what you're saying. Otherwise, no one will believe you.

How do you sound to others? Is your voice pleasing to listen to, or is it harsh or annoying? Can people hear what you're saying or must they strain just to hear you? Are you speaking fast enough to hold their interest, but not too fast for them to keep up? Are you oozing confidence or revealing uncertainty? Do you come across as being sincere or as being a phony? Do you act like you're better than them or like you're one of them?

Ideally, you should be speaking loud enough to be heard (no whispering or mumbling), but not too loud (no yelling or screaming); you should slow down so they can keep up, but not to a crawl; you should speak in a lower pitch (a deeper voice), which is more soothing to others; and you should avoid long pauses in between thoughts (no "uhs" or "you knows.")

And how, uh, do you act, uh, when you're talking? Do you say one thing, but by your body language, say something else? While your lips are moving, is your body moving in sync?

I must tell you that your co-workers and your customers will be watching your every move—the tone of your voice, the look on your face, and the way your body moves. The problem with this is that reading body language is not an exact science, and your co-workers and customers are not exactly scientists, which means that what you say will be wide open to interpretation.

Whenever there is room for interpretation, there is opportunity for misinterpretation. So, when you fold your arms, people might think you're being defensive; when you cover your mouth while speaking, they might think you're being dishonest; when you tap your foot while they're speaking, they might think you're being impatient; and when you grit your teeth, clench your fist, and turn beet red, they might think you're mad. Now, maybe you are being defensive, dishonest, impatient, or angry, but then, maybe you're not. The point is that you need to be aware of what you're doing.

Remove all barriers to effective communication. There are many things that can block effective communication. These barriers can be environmental distractions, mental distractions, or personal differences. All must be dealt with.

Environmental distractions would include things like poor lighting, loud or repetitive noises, extreme temperatures, uncomfortable seating, cramped spaces, limited time, people who are too odd or ugly to look at, people who are too beautiful to stop looking at, or people who have annoying habits.

Mental distractions would be distractions to either you or the person you are talking to, and would include bad attitudes, such as "Who cares what you or your kind think?" or "What could you possibly have to say that could be more important than what I have to say?" or emotions, such as love, which, as it turns out, can be both blind and deaf, or preoccupations with other things, such as "Did I leave the door unlocked?" "Did I leave my keys in the car?" "What did he mean when he said that?" "Is she going to call?" "Is it going to rain this weekend?" "Will Rachel marry Ross?" or, "Does everybody really love Raymond?"

Personal differences can be age related, cultural, educational, intellectual, or linguistic. In a workplace that is becoming as diverse as the world outside of it, differences will become more common, and the need to bridge those differences will become more urgent.

Distractions can be removed, and differences can be overcome. Sometimes, it will be easy, and sometimes not. When it's not that easy, it will take a greater commitment on your part to make it work. Somebody has to make that commitment and take that responsibility; somebody has to stop playing that childish game of "I will if you will." That somebody might as well be you. You're the one who wants to be happy and successful, aren't you?

Take responsibility for reaching an understanding. Whenever you want something, it becomes your responsibility to get it. It's no different when you're talking to people. If you want someone to understand something, you can't just hope that he understands, you must help him to understand; if you want someone to agree with you, you can't just expect him to agree, you must convince him to agree; if you want someone to change what he's doing, you can't just wish for him to change, you must motivate him to change.

If he doesn't understand, agree, change, or do whatever it is that you want him to do, it's up to you to change whatever you're doing or saying until he does understand, agree, change, or do what you want. If he's not hearing you, you must speak up; if he's not listening to you, you must get his attention; if he's not understanding you, you must explain better; if there are barriers present, you must remove them; and if there's absolutely no way that you're going to get through to him, you must realize that it's time to stop talking.

Have I gotten through to you? Are you convinced of the importance of being able to communicate effectively? Do you understand that without effective communication, you would be hard pressed to convince anyone to do anything; you would be unable to ask for help or show appreciation for the help you get; you would be unable to learn from others or to teach them what you know; you would be unable to give or get feedback about performance; you would have difficulty dealing with change; you would find working as a team to be nearly impossible; and, you would never be happy and successful at work.

Do you like to hear your co-workers saying, "You should have said something," "You could have made yourself clearer," "I don't remember you saying that," "I didn't hear you," "I wasn't paying attention," or, "Did you say something?" Or, would you rather hear them saying, "I hear you loud and clear," or "I understand what you're saying?" So let me ask you this—do you understand the words that are coming out of my mouth?

SUMMARY

- Anything that can be misunderstood will be misunderstood.

- The key to effective communication is understanding, and you are the key to understanding.
- It helps to know what you're doing or what you're saying before you do or say anything.
- Without effective communication, businesses wouldn't prosper, teams wouldn't function, and you wouldn't be happy or successful.

Assignments:

1. From now on,
- Think about what you're going to say.
- Say what you think.
- Say what you have to say.
- Say what you mean.
- Mean what you say.
- Say less; listen more.
- Say it in a nice way.
- Say it loud and clear.
- Say it before it's too late.
- Say hello to the people you meet.
- Say thanks to the people who help.
- Say it, don't spray it.

Lesson Sixteen:
Managing People

<u>Objectives:</u>

1. To understand the keys to being a successful manager.

Once upon a time, a long, long time ago, I did some management training. That was before I decided to focus my attention on helping workers. As I saw it, there were already more than enough people training managers. I have nothing against managers, being one myself. Actually, I think I'm doing them a favor by helping to train their employees. Any smart manager would be thrilled to have employees who came to work with an excellent work ethic and the basic skills needed to perform at their best. Any manager who doesn't make programs like *Working 101* available to his employees is making a big mistake, in my "unbiased" opinion.

I'm including this lesson because as workers start to perform better, many of them will find themselves being promoted into supervisory positions, and I don't want them to fail, and because there are many lower level supervisors and managers out there who lack some very basic management training.

There's something you should know, whether you're a new supervisor or an experienced one. Regardless of what your title is, how long you've had it, or how much you get paid to do it, as long as you're getting a paycheck from somebody else, you're still an employee of the company. As such, it's just as important for you to develop the basic, soft work skills as it is for anyone else. In fact, it may be even more important for you.

You're a role model for your employees, whether you know it or not, and whether you like it or not. Your employees will be watching every move you make, listening to every word you say (except, of course, when you want them to do something), and trying to make sense of it all (but not always being successful at doing that.) The point is that if you're going to be a role model anyway, you might as well be a good one.

A good supervisor, therefore, will:

- Learn the basic skills.
- Make sure his employees learn them.
- Recognize and reward those employees who use these skills.
- Encourage those who are not using them to start using them.

This brings me to what I believe to be the twelve most important things a manager needs to know (in no particular order):

1. **The more you teach and encourage employees to do well, the less you have to criticize or discipline them for doing poorly.** As a manager, your focus needs to be on teaching and encouraging workers to do better. In my opinion, you can never do too much training, but you better be sure that you're doing enough. I can assure you that any time you spend on training will be time well spent, and any money that you spend

Mike Jacobs

up front on training will, almost invariably, cost less than what it's going to cost if you don't do the training. The mistakes alone that untrained workers will make are going to kill you.

2. **Criticism should be given only to help employees to improve their performance, and never to hurt or humiliate them.** No one likes to be criticized, but sometimes they need it. In fact, to let a worker believe that he is doing a good job when he is not would be inherently unfair to him. The purpose of criticism, however, should always be to develop people, not to destroy them; to build people up, not to tear them down. Its focus should be on behaviors, not on people. Its initiation should be on facts, not on hearsay, rumors, or accusations. Its presentation should be in private, not in public.

3. **A manager's focus or emphasis should be on looking for the good in his workers while not overlooking the bad.** Recognition of what one's workers are doing is crucial. If good behaviors are to be repeated, they must be recognized, and if bad behaviors are to be eliminated, they too must be recognized. Of course, no behaviors can be recognized if managers choose to sit in their offices all day.

4. **What supervisors get from their employees is in direct proportion to what they give to their employees.** They can give employees what they need to perform well—support, supplies, fair wages, recognition, feedback, time, attention, training, thanks...or they can give employees what will cause them to perform poorly—undue pressure, harsh criticism, reprimands,

intimidation, or a lack of any of the things they need.

5. **The wise manager does not feel challenged by excellent employees, but is grateful for them**. Managers may do certain tasks, such as writing reports, attending meetings, and conducting interviews, but ultimately, they are judged, not by what they do, but by what their employees do. Managers, therefore, are only as good as their employees make them look, and should be very appreciative of the ones who make them look good.

6. **It is not the style of your management that counts, but the results of it.** Whatever works in any given situation is best. During the course of a day, one might use several different styles, depending on circumstances. If the results are there, how can anyone question the style?

7. **Managers need to have some control over their employees.** Too much control, however, will stifle creativity and fuel discontent; too little, on the other hand, will stifle productivity and invite chaos. A good middle ground must be found, but one way or another, there must be some control.

8. **If you have to tell employees that you're the boss, you're not a very good one.** Respect is to be commanded, not demanded from your employees. Respect is not something that comes with a title; it is earned by one's actions.

9. **An employee who is doing poorly is not necessarily incapable of doing better.** If an employee is doing poorly, unless you have given him everything he needs, you are partially responsible

for his poor performance. If you have given him everything he needs to perform better, and he still performs poorly, you must ask yourself why he is still working for you. I'll further suggest to you that if you have poor performers still working for you, you also have some not so happy good performers. (I have to share a little story with you. My godfather and mentor, Sam, once shared with me, in his wonderful southern drawl, the "chicken salad" theory of managing poor performers. He told me that you can't make chicken salad out of chicken shit no matter how much mayonnaise you use. Now, before you get all upset with me, remember that he said it, not me. If it would make you feel better, I'll tell you that I haven't been able to eat chicken salad since then, and I'm deeply sorry if it has the same affect on you.)

10. **Managers who are never thankful to employees who offer suggestions or who offer to help, have employees who never offer suggestions and never offer to help.** You must be thankful that they give, or they'll stop giving. Even if their ideas are silly and their help is not helpful, you still have to thank them for giving it. You never want to close out this important resource.

11. **Good workers are good workers, no matter what they look like, and good ideas are good ideas, no matter who came up with them.** A good supervisor will use the best workers and the best ideas no matter what. Prejudices, preconceived notions, grudges, selfishness, and pride should have no place in a manager's decision regarding his employees and their ideas.

12. **Managers are representatives of the company.** As such, they must support the company enthusiastically and never criticize it to employees. Managers must always look out for their employees, but never at the expense of the company.

SUMMARY

• Managers must develop the same basic, soft work skills that all workers need to develop, and in addition, must follow several important practices that will ensure their success.

Assignments:

1. Choose any one of the twelve suggestions above and try it for a week.
2. Enjoy a good chicken salad sandwich.

Lesson Seventeen:
Dealing with Change

<u>Objectives:</u>

1. To accept that change will happen, and that it's good for you.
2. To understand how the workplace is changing.
3. To learn how to handle change.
4. To learn how to initiate change.

God grant me the serenity to accept
the things I cannot change, the
courage to change the things I can,
and the wisdom to know the difference.
—Reinhold Neibuhr's Serenity Prayer

If there's one thing we can be sure of, other than death, it's that we can't be sure of anything. Everything changes, as we're constantly being reminded—"nothing lasts forever," "here today, gone tomorrow," "This too shall pass," "You never know," and, "A change is in the air." Yes, the times, they are a' changing, and with that, the seasons will change, people will change, jobs will change, people will change jobs, the workplace will change, the rules will change, opinions will change, attitudes will change, statistics will change, the weather will change, and a great many diapers will get changed. Unless you're putting money in a vending machine, you can always expect change, and, you can never assume anything.

It's been estimated that employees will spend at least 50% of their time dealing with change at work. This is not because the good folks in upper management have been sitting around all day just thinking of ways to keep workers on their toes; it's because change happens! Change is a natural and necessary fact of life, and a necessary part of doing business. Change is good; it's good for business, and it's good for you.

So, if you know what's good for you, you'll accept change, and you'll learn to deal with it and live with it. And don't let anybody tell you that it's only human to resist change. Perhaps we humans have some inclination to resist it, but we don't have to follow our inclinations. We can choose not to resist. The choice is as clear as it could be – you can either embrace change or be made obsolete by it.

A change is in the air

There's a change in the air. At work, you're changing, your co-workers are changing, your job is changing, and the workplace, itself, is changing.

You're getting older, and hopefully wiser; you're learning new things and gaining valuable experience; your values, opinions, and perspectives are being shaped and reshaped; and your body is changing as it ages and endures the daily wear and tear that it takes.

Your co-workers are changing in much the same way. Day by day, and in some cases, minute by minute, they're changing their opinions, their moods, and their minds.

Your job is changing as you work with new co-workers, new technologies, new managers, new budgets, new policies and procedures, new expectations, new deadlines, new customers, new tasks, new responsibilities, and new objectives.

The workplace is changing as the workforce changes and becomes more diverse, as work conditions improve, as consumers become more knowledgeable and more demanding, as competition for jobs intensifies, as technology marches on, as globalization becomes a fact of life, and as new books come out with even more advice on how to change.

As you change, you must adapt by keeping your mind and body in shape, by using your experience as a means to improve, by acquiring the skills that you'll need, and by believing in yourself. As your co-workers change, you must try to understand what they're going through, and help them to get through it, and you must learn how to interrelate, cooperate, and communicate with them. As your job and the workplace change, you must form the habits and acquire the skills that will help you to first survive, and then to thrive in this ever changing workplace.

The workplace today

It sure ain't what it used to be. So much has changed, and so much more remains to be changed. I want to take some time here to talk in greater detail about the changes that are happening in the workplace. It's important that you understand them because you will be greatly affected by them. If you can't learn to deal with these changes, it will not be long before you're changing jobs or standing on the unemployment line. Remember, you can't be successful at a job you no longer have.

The ten changes that I believe are having the greatest impact on business and on your job, are, in no particular order of importance:

1. The workforce is becoming more diverse.
2. Working conditions are improving.
3. Businesses are getting leaner and more efficient.
4. Productivity is rising, as are expectations that it will continue to do so.
5. Consumers are becoming more knowledgeable and more demanding.
6. Technology is changing faster than ever before.
7. Globalization is changing the way we do business.
8. Businesses are learning how to spend money more effectively.
9. Competition for jobs is heating up.
10. New management philosophies are gaining popularity.

The workforce is becoming more diverse. According to the Families and Work Institute, today's workforce has greater gender balance, is older, better educated, and more racially and ethnically diverse. More women, minorities, and younger adults are entering the workforce, and more older adults are either staying in longer or re-entering it.

Today, more than 50% of the workforce are women. Fifty years ago, it was only 30%. According to the Department of Labor, about 45% of managers now are women, and when you look at the growing trend of women graduating from college, you can see how that percentage will continue to grow.

DID YOU KNOW? Over six million women now run their own businesses.

Today, there are some 70 million workers over the age of forty, and it is estimated that in 2010, more than half of the workforce was over forty years old. With people living longer than ever before and the birth rate remaining steady, the population will continue to age, and so too will the workforce.

Today, with graduation rates from high schools and colleges on the increase, the workforce is better educated, or so you would think. I, myself, am not so sure of it. I see the diplomas, but I'm not seeing the good sense; I see the technical and computer skills, but I'm not seeing the basic, soft skills that are in such demand. I'm seeing too many kids coming out of school who can't read or write, and don't even know their ABC's, let alone their IPR's.

I'm not the only one seeing this, either. Kenneth J. Cooper, in an article for the Washington Post, wrote, "Three quarters of the nation's school children are unable to compose a well organized, coherent essay, a skill frequently demanded in the modern workplace.

In my home state, the Washington Education Foundation interviewed key employers and educators across the state, and consistently heard comments about how graduates lacked certain verbal and communication skills, and had difficulty integrating those skills into the workplace; about how new workers lacked any real work ethic, and lacked the basic work skills such as how to come to work, to be on time, to know how to dress and to know what was expected of them in the workplace; and about how they lacked employability and the ability to solve problems, make decisions, and get along as members of a team.

This is not a Washington state problem, but a problem we're facing across this country and around the world.

Today, there are more people of different races and different nationalities working together in the workplace. The "melting pot" has, indeed, spilled over into the workforce.

Today, unions have less influence than they did in the 1950's when they reached the height of their influence. The enactment of laws that protect workers, the reduction of jobs in manufacturing, and the realization by managers that happy and successful workers are productive workers, have all contributed to this decline.

DID YOU KNOW? In the 1950's, union membership was 35% of the workforce; today, it's less than 15%.

What does all this diversity mean to business? It means a growing pool from which to draw good workers who bring with them new ideas, new perspectives, new energies, and new sensitivities. And as employers begin to see the benefits that diversity brings, they will begin to understand that good workers are good workers, no matter how they look, and that good ideas are good ideas, no matter who they came from.

Of course, there's a downside. As men and women mix, there will surely be more socialization; as people of different races and nations mix, there will surely be more harassment and discrimination; as younger and older workers mix, there will surely be more distrust; as more and more workers come together, there will surely be more conflict. And please don't misunderstand me; I'm not trying to offend anyone or make any judgments about people; I'm merely trying to report what I see.

Working conditions are improving. Most of us don't work in sweatshops anymore. Today, workplaces are safer and cleaner, thanks, in large part, to the passage of several labor laws; hours worked are shorter, down from an average of 50 hours a week in the 1930's

Mike Jacobs

to around 43 hours a week today; and wages and benefits are higher than ever before.

NEWSFLASH: It's not all good news. The workplace may be a lot safer, but it is not as safe as it could be. Lots of workers are still getting hurt on the job; some are still dying on it. The number of hours worked may have come down, but they are starting to go back up because employers are demanding more productivity and employees are needing more money to pay their bills. Wages and benefits may be higher, but raises are starting to get lower. For the last three years in a row, the average annual increase has been less than 4%. Many workers are having their wages frozen temporarily, and many more are getting no increase at all. Some are having their wages cut. Given the steady growth of inflation, our purchasing power is not keeping pace with our increased wages.

DID YOU KNOW? In 2003, the average wage of CEO's increased by 27%. Today, this disparity continues.

And the bad news continues—Job security is not what it used to be. While employers continue to sing the praises of loyalty to the company, they're singing a different tune when it comes to being loyal to their employees. They're cutting their costs by laying off workers, outsourcing jobs, encouraging early retirements, and using more of what they call contingent workers. (part-time and temporary help) I don't even want to think about what they might do when robots become more practical and more cost effective.

I don't mean to scare you. It's not all that bad. Actually, we are better off than we've ever been. We've clearly benefited from the laws that have been passed, from the unions that have represented us, and from our employers who have finally figured out that it pays to make us happy.

It's up to us now to do the very best jobs we can do so we can be safer, work fewer hours, make more money, and be more secure in our jobs. Your employer will take good of you if you do a good job, and he'll do this, not because it's good for you, but because it's good for business. But that's okay. As long as you're taken care of, why should you care what his motivations are?

Businesses are getting leaner and more efficient. Tougher competition from here and abroad, consumer demand, and the escalating costs of doing business are forcing businesses to reexamine their operations. They see the need to provide better quality products and services at lower costs.

Now, if you were a business owner, and you wanted to be more efficient, what would you do? Would you raise prices? Not if you wanted your customers to still do business with you. You might be able to raise them some if you have to cover rising costs, but you can only raise them so high. Would you cut costs then? Probably, but which costs would you cut? Where would you look for the efficiencies you need?

You would look at your payroll, because that's where most of your costs are, and because from the biggest costs come the biggest savings. To accomplish this, you could do one or more of three things—

1. Reduce the number of employees you have.
2. Spend less on your employees.
3. Get more productivity from your employees.

Being the great humanitarians that they are, most employers are doing all three. In spite of the fact that, as Dr. Kelley observed, you "can't boost productivity by laying people off and scaring them," businesses are still laying people off. It's not as bad as it used to be, but it's bad enough. Layoffs still remain an option for today's businesses.

DID YOU KNOW? In 2011, 20,041,000 workers were laid off. (Another 23,083,000 quit their jobs.) These are not small numbers.

For those workers fortunate enough not to be laid off, there are other sacrifices to be made. The costs to businesses of wages and benefits are either being cut or shifted to the workers. With "cost shifting," workers can still have their benefits, but they have to pay more to have them. Here are some things that businesses are doing along these lines—

- They're cutting back or freezing wages.
- They're requiring workers to make larger contributions to their health care and retirement plans, plans that have higher deductibles and lower maximum payouts.

DID YOU KNOW? In 2001, in companies with more than 500 employees, 30% of employees still had no health care coverage through the company. Many today still have no coverage.

- They're switching from pension plans that have guaranteed payouts to 401K plans with varying payouts that are determined by worker choice and economic conditions.

- They're offering early retirement plans for long term workers with higher wages.
- They're offering less vacation, holiday, and sick day benefits, and not allowing workers to accumulate or cash out their days. It's use it or lose it, baby.
- They're hiring more part-time and temporary workers who don't qualify for benefits, reducing hours of full-time workers, and eliminating unauthorized overtime.
- They're outsourcing jobs overseas to people who will do the same jobs we do for a lot less money. (more on this a little later.)

And, they're expecting workers to do more.

Productivity is rising, as are expectations that it will continue to do so. They're expecting more, and we're doing more. The American worker is the most productive worker in the world, but, we are not as productive as we could be. So when our employers are asking for more, they're not asking for too much. They're not asking us to do more than we're capable of doing, and they have every right to ask.

Not only can we do more, but the truth is that we have not been fully responsible for the increased productivity that we have seen in recent years. In an article for Newsweek, entitled, "Men at Overwork," Brad Stone suggests that there are four things that have contributed to increased productivity—1. An intense focus by businesses on keeping costs under control; 2. The outsourcing of jobs overseas to take advantage of cheaper labor markets; 3. Improving marketing and research tools, including digital media, cell phones, e-mail, and

Mike Jacobs

faxes; and, 4. Increased expectations by management, requiring workers to work longer and harder.

Nowhere does he say anything about worker improvement. Does that mean we haven't improved? Apparently not enough. We are working more, however, putting in more overtime and taking fewer days off, simply because there's too much work to get done. It's almost as if we were afraid to go home and leave the work undone for fear that our employers will find someone else to do the work.

DID YOU KNOW? The average American worker takes less than three weeks of vacation each year, compared with his European counterpart who takes an average of more than six weeks each year. A recent survey that was done found that 63% of workers here wanted to work fewer hours but were afraid to do so.

DID YOU KNOW? An Accenture online survey of 4,100 executives in 33 countries found that 75% of them either frequently or occasionally do work during paid time off. I can assure you that they're not the only ones doing so.

The expectations of greater productivity will not soon go away. Bosses are not going to wake up some day and think, "Gee, I think we're about as productive as we need to be. I think I'll send a memo to my employees asking them to slow down." I can see it now—

Memo to Employees

It has come to our attention that productivity has reached an all time high. We do appreciate your efforts, but we must ask that you not be any more productive.

The higher profits that have been made as a result of your increased productivity have created an unexpected dilemma for the company. We simply don't know what to do with all this money. This has created a severe strain on our accounting department and has brought about inquiries from the I.R.S. To assist you with this new initiative, we will be offering paid days off to employees who are otherwise unable to be less productive. Management.

Yeah, right, and pigs will soon be flying.

Consumers are becoming more knowledgeable and more demanding. In the 1940's and early 1950's, after World War II, making babies became a popular thing to do. Today, those babies are all grown up. They're hard working, well educated, and sophisticated people with lots and lots of money to spend, and their own babies are babies no more. They, too, have money to spend.

These are not your gullible, accepting, timid customers of the past. These people know what they want, they know what you have to offer, they know what their options are, they have lots of options, and they want what they want and they want it now. They didn't get their money handed to them on a silver platter, and they're not about to hand it over to you for nothing. You can fool these customers once, but they won't be your customers anymore.

Technology is changing faster than ever before. It's tough for people like me. If I want to watch a movie on a DVD, my wife has to set it up; if I want to put a phone number on speed dial on my cell phone, my daughter has to do it; and if I want to fix a problem on my computer, my son has to fix it for me. I have all the new gadgets; I just don't know what to do with them. I'm trying, but it's not easy being me.

In the workplace we're using all this technology that even five or ten years ago, we didn't have. For workers who can master these things, it makes life so much easier, but for workers who can't, it makes life miserable. For many workers, the accessibility that comes from these devices makes it harder to get away from their work.

Five or ten years from now, what thingamajigs will we be using? Nuclear powered copiers? Laser disintegrating shredders? Teleportation devices? Robots? Flying pigs?

All I can say is "beam me up Scotty." I'm ready for retirement.

Globalization is changing the way we do business. Disney was right; it is a small world after all. Globalization is changing the way we do business, as well as the types of businesses we do. It has greatly expanded our markets for buying, selling, and producing goods, and has vastly increased the available labor pool; it has moved our country from its emphasis on manufacturing to a new emphasis on the provision of services and information; and, it has changed us from being self sufficient to being reliant on other countries, as they are on us. Perhaps the biggest impact on workers in this country has been the outsourcing of jobs overseas. It was bound to happen. Businesses could not overlook the huge savings to be had from cheap labor in other countries. And don't sell these people in other countries short either. They may be cheap, but they're not stupid, and they really need the money, so they're willing to work hard for it.

Outsourcing started with jobs requiring manual labor, but it has now spread to many white collar jobs as well, including computer technicians, customer service representatives, researchers, data analysts, and telemarketers. Countries like India have the skilled workers to fill these jobs at very low wages, and they're teaching them English, which makes it even more attractive to American businesses.

DID YOU KNOW? Forrester Research estimates that within 15 years, some 3.3 million service jobs will be filled by workers in other countries.

Before you go and call your congressman, you have to know that the news is not all doom and gloom. The Information and Technology Association of America predicts that the outsourcing trend will ultimately lower inflation, create new jobs here, and boost productivity in America. Besides, many businesses are beginning to realize that once you factor in some other costs, the savings are not as great. The U.S., in fact, is looking more and more attractive to both foreign and domestic companies, given the cheap dollar, the low energy costs, the highly productive workers, and the relative stability of the economy. And one more thing to consider is that many jobs from overseas are being "insourced" right here. Numerous foreign companies are opening manufacturing plants right here in the good old U.S.A., creating new jobs for American workers. So chill out.

Businesses are learning how to spend money more effectively. Businesses know that they have to spend money to make money. They also know that along the way, some money will be wasted. It's all part of the costs of doing business. But that doesn't mean that they're going to just willingly give it away and chalk it up to experience. No, they're going to do whatever they can to keep their losses down to manageable amounts.

Mike Jacobs

They know, for instance, that there will always be some costs associated with absenteeism, tardiness, turnover, on the job injuries, theft and destruction of company property, and equipment downtime caused by worker incompetence or indifference.

DID YOU KNOW? The average cost just to replace one worker ranges from $3,000 to $13,000. In some cases, it is much higher.

What they're starting to realize, though, is that when not controlled, these costs can become excessive, and that's unacceptable. So, they're now spending more money on ways to prevent and/or control these costs. This has not been easy for them, because they can't easily put a number on what these things are costing them, and without that number, right there in black and white, staring them in the face, they feel very uncomfortable in spending more. They're afraid of throwing good money away on programs that might not work.

To their surprise, they are learning that money well spent is often the best way to save money, and that the costs of prevention are almost always less than, and better spent than, the costs of intervention.

Therefore, you shouldn't be surprised when they start introducing more job screening, drug testing, counseling, psychological testing, security and surveillance programs, wellness programs, and training programs. Get yourself ready, my friend, because "big brother" will soon be watching, if he's not already doing so.

Competition for jobs is heating up. For the past few years, our national unemployment rate has been running between eight to ten percent. Recently, it has fallen to 7.5% and this has given many people a false sense of security, thinking that with more people having jobs, there won't be as many out looking for one. Nothing could be further from the truth. There is now, as there has always been, a fierce competition for the jobs that people want to work. In case you didn't know,

DID YOU KNOW?

- A 7.5% unemployment rate means that there are approximately twelve million people unemployed.
- Every day, more young adults are entering the workforce and more older adults are re-entering it.
- Approximately two million people are not looking for work right now because they don't think that there's anything out there for them, but tomorrow, they may change their minds.
- Some ten million workers now have more than one job, and every day, more people are doing the same thing.
- There are 140 million workers in the civilian workforce today and at least half of them are not happy with their jobs. They're just waiting for something better to come along, something, perhaps, like your job.

New management philosophies are gaining popularity. Every year, it seems there's a new management craze that's sweeping the nation and topping the best-seller list.

There was Theory X, Theory Y, and, of course, Theory Z, and there was KITA (Kick 'Em in the Ass), TQM (Total Quality Management), Re-engineering, MBWA (Management by Walking Around), and a host of other abbreviations too long to mention (even if I were to abbreviate them.)

Managers have learned how to form quality circles, manage in only one minute, shift their paradigms, and travel up the organization. They have gotten advice on management from all sorts of people including Attila the Hun, and even from Jesus Christ, CEO. Heck, they've even heard advice from a few mice, a peacock and some penguins, and a bowl full of fish.

Don't get me wrong, some of these have given managers some good advice. And managers are soaking this stuff up like a sponge, and using it on you know who. The problem with this is that some managers, perhaps too many of them, don't know how to put these ideas into practice. I knew this one manager who you'd swear thought MBWA meant management by walking away. I knew others who managed to walk around, but never saw anything. They might as well have had their eyes closed. This one manager I had was such a jerk. He took that KITA stuff literally and would go around actually kicking people in the butt. He thought he was being funny, but when people started to complain, he was fired. I guess you could say that it came back to BITA (Bite him in the Ass.)

I'm sorry, I just couldn't help myself. I had to say it. Forgive me. Seriously, the basic gist of most of these philosophies is that workers should be given greater responsibilities to make their own decisions, solve their own problems, and form their own teams.

What does all this mean to you?

It means that doing "good enough" will no longer be good enough. No longer will mediocrity be acceptable. Your co-workers won't appreciate it; your boss won't tolerate it; and your customers won't stay around for it.

It means that you will have to learn to get along with others by tolerating their differences, understanding their beliefs, accepting their ideas, listening to their opinions, and cooperating fully with them. If you have any prejudices, you'll have to leave them at home.

It means you will have to develop the skills needed to provide the best service and process the best information—communications, problem solving, decision making, interpersonal relations, and all of the other skills taught in *Working 101*.

It means you must be more productive, help to control costs, learn new technologies, and get to know your products better than your customers know them, and your customers better than they know themselves.

It means you should stop worrying about things like layoffs and outsourcing, and focus your attention, instead, on doing your job.

And, it means that you need to learn how to deal with change.

When change happens

When change happens, what will you do? When your boss says, "There's going to be some changes around here," will your first urge be to resist, and to say something (not to his face, of course) like "What now?" "Are you kidding me?" "Is he for real?" "Did I do something to deserve this?" or if you're having a really bad day, "No blanking way; they can take this blanking job and shove it. Do you think he heard me?"

Will you do, as so many of your co-workers do, and look for reasons not to change? "It's not broken, so why fix it?" "It can't be done." "We've always done it this way." "This isn't the right time." "There isn't enough time." "We've got too much to do as it is." "Why not leave well enough alone?" "Why change now?" "Why can't we wait?"

There's not one good reason among them to not change. Do you want to know why your co-workers really don't want to change? No, it's not laziness, although there is some of that going on; its fear and comfort that keep them from changing, fear of what they don't know and comfort with what they do know. They like to have things just the way they are, even if it's not the ideal way to have them. They get used to things and develop habits that are not easily broken. They may find themselves in a rut, but it's their rut, and they're staying in it, for better or for worse.

They don't want to change, and they don't believe that they could even if they wanted to. After all, "You can't teach an old dog new tricks," and "A leopard never changes his spots." Right? These good folks are content just to put in their eight hours and be left alone. As Studs Terkel wrote, they are "walking wounded," and "surviving the day." And it's best just to let them be. As Woodrow Wilson observed, "If you want to make enemies, try to change something."

What happens to these people when change does happen? Well, it's not very pretty. You see, by resisting change, they make themselves obsolete, and a ready target to someday be replaced by someone more willing to change. They certainly don't make any friends in high places. Bosses are not very fond of people who resist their ideas, especially without even trying them first.

Listen to me, and listen good—you are not a dog or a leopard, or a mouse, peacock, penguin, or fish, for that matter, and you don't deserve to be "walking wounded." God gave you the ability to control your own thoughts, actions, and emotions, and now, you can use that ability to decide not to resist. You can't resist, anyway. The handwriting, or I should say, the graffiti, is on the wall—change is coming, and you'll have to choose to either come along for the ride, or to just go away.

Changing

As my mother was shoving vegetables down my throat (a long time ago), she would tell me, "Try it; you might like it," and "It's not going to kill you to eat it." Well, I'm still here, and now I love my veggies and they love me. I've since learned that you can get used to just about anything. As the saying goes, "After you live in a zoo long enough, you stop smelling the animals."

Nothing they can change at work is going to kill you, and like my veggies, will probably make your life at work better. Just give it a chance. Become what I like to call, an "agent of change." This is a person who:

- Accepts that change will happen.
- Believes that change should happen.
- Knows that change is good.
- Knows that he must work with change.
- Is willing to make personal change.
- Is eager to initiate change.
- Is committed to ensuring that all changes that should be made, are made, and that all changes that are made, are made to work.

Change will happen, it should happen because it's good for business, and the change will do you good as

well. The only sensible thing to do, therefore, is to work with change to see that it works. This much we know.

Are you willing, however, to make personal changes? Are you willing to form new habits, take new actions, think new thoughts, make new choices, accept new ideas, see things from new perspectives, meet new people, make new friends, try new things, learn new skills, wear new clothes, cut your hair, lose twenty pounds, or do whatever it takes to succeed?

You may have to work harder and smarter than you've ever worked before, take on added responsibilities, and make some personal sacrifices. You may have to change your attitude from being negative to being positive, your behaviors from being hurtful to being helpful, and your habits from being bad to being good. If you know what's good for you, you'll do this sooner, not later. Later, it might be too late.

Of bad habits, Horace Fletcher said, "The underlying cause of all weakness and unhappiness in man has always been, and still is, weak habit of thought." Bad habits can kill you. At work, they can destroy any chance you might have of being happy and successful. Bad habits must be changed, and they can be changed. Somewhere in your past, you made a bad choice, and you've been making it over and over again, to the point where it has become a bad habit. You can now make a better choice, and make it over and over again until it becomes a new and improved habit.

Initiating change

How would you like to never again have your boss tell you that things are going to change? You would? Then change them yourself. What better way to use your initiative than to use it to make changes? Who better to make them than you? Who knows (or should know) your job better than you know it? Why waste time waiting to be told?

What can you change? Better still, what can you not change? Nothing at work is sacred. Anything can be done better, faster, slower, easier, smarter, sooner, later, more efficiently, more effectively, or more conveniently. Anything can be made bigger, smaller, cheaper, stronger, harder, softer, lighter, heavier, better, or better looking. If something is broken, it can be fixed, and if it's not broken, it still can be made better.

Everything is open to change—policies and procedures can be changed; forms can be changed; assignments can be changed; schedules can be changed; performance standards can be changed; teams can be changed; budgets can be changed; management can be changed; co-workers can be changed; minds can be changed; jobs can be changed; priorities can be changed; you can be changed; and names can be changed to protect the innocent. (Sorry, I got a little carried away.)

In lesson thirteen, we learned how to simplify tasks and modify how they're done; in lesson fourteen, we learned how to ask certain questions that will lead to progress. This is how you initiate change. Try it, you might like it. It wouldn't kill you to change. (That's for you, mom.)

Working with change

What if somebody else initiates the change? What if your boss does tell you that things are going to change, whether you like it or not? What do you do then?

You don't resist, and you don't do it poorly just because you don't like doing it. A half hearted, "I'll do it if I have to, but I don't like doing it, so I won't do it well," attitude is not going to cut it. It's not fair to your boss, and it's not good for you.

When changes need to be made, your job is to help make them work. To do this, you must:

1. Find out what you can about the change—what needs to be done, who's going to do it, what your role is going to be, how it will affect you, why it's being made…Being informed will help you to overcome any fears you may have and any discomfort you may be feeling.

2. Give it a chance to work. You can't say it won't work if you've never tried it. Not all changes will work, and your boss will be okay with you saying, "I tried it, but it won't work." That's a lot different from you saying, "I won't try it because it won't work."

3. Give it time to work. With most organizational changes, there will be, at first, some confusion, problems, mistakes, and misunderstandings, none of which are good reasons to give up on something. Eventually, the kinks can be worked out, and with time and familiarity, acceptance will come.

4. Change again if you must. Rest assured that if changes don't work, they can always be changed again, sometimes even back to the way things were before. In fact, odds are they will change again. Nothing that changes in the workplace can be so bad that you can't adapt to it and live with it, and nothing, no matter how bad

it is, will last forever. With all things, someday, if you're still there, you'll be able to look back and say, "Remember when...?"

SUMMARY

- Change is inevitable, it is necessary, and it is good.
- It is not natural to resist change; it's merely a choice to be made.
- If you give change a chance and a little time to work, you will know if it works. If it works, you're better off, and if it doesn't work, you can change again. (And you've learned something in the bargain.)
- If you don't change, you will become obsolete.

Assignments:

1. Tomorrow, commit to making at least one change at work. Here are a few suggestions you might want to consider:
- Change the route you take to work.
- Change your attitude about work.
- Change the way you look at people.
- Change the way you do your job.
- Change the people you hang out with.
- Change a bad habit.
- Change the way you spend your time.
- Change your mind about people you don't like.
- Change your priorities.
- Change the page; this lesson is over.

Lesson Eighteen: Handling Adversity

<u>Objectives:</u>

1. To accept the fact that you will face adversity.
2. To resolve to overcome whatever obstacles you may face.
3. To understand the benefits of facing up to your obstacles and the consequences of walking away.

The road to success is always under construction.
—Anonymous

On the road to success, you will face adversity. At times, you may feel like giving up, like you can't take it anymore, like there's just no use in trying. You may even think of yourself as being unworthy of success.

Depressed? Well, don't be, because everyone faces adversity at one time or another. All successful people have faced it, overcome it, and become stronger by it. Many of them owe their success to their ability to overcome the obstacles that life has put in their path.

Now I also know that the sadness and setbacks of my life are not unique to me. Even the wisest and most successful of this world suffer chapters of heartbreak and failure but they, unlike me, have learned that there is no peace without trouble, no rest without strain, no laughter without sorrow, no victory without struggle and that is the price we all pay for living.—Og Mandino

If obstacles are the bad news, the good news is that there are few obstacles that cannot be overcome with a little faith, hard work, creativity, persistence, and enthusiasm. Even those that can't be overcome can still make you a better person for having tried. You have to at least try to overcome any obstacles. As singer Beverly Sills once said, "You may be disappointed if you fail, but you are doomed if you don't try." And what if you're disappointed? So what? There's always a next time.

When faced with adversity, you have nothing to lose, and everything to gain by at least trying to overcome it. Your resolve must be strong, and as the obstacles grow bigger, your resolve must grow stronger—when the work gets harder, resolve to work a little harder at it; when time is running out, resolve to work a little faster; when money or supplies are running low, resolve to be a little more creative or economical with their use; when a customer or co-worker is being rude or ignorant, resolve to be a little more understanding; and when things are not going the way you'd like them to go, resolve to be a little more patient. A little more of anything won't kill you.

Tell that to some of your co-workers. Apparently, it's killing them, because when the work gets harder, they stop to complain; when the time's running out, they stop to complain; when money or supplies are running out, they stop to complain; when things are not going their way, they stop to complain. In fact, the only time they don't stop to complain is when a customer or co-worker is being rude or ignorant. Then, they go out of their way to show that they can be a little more rude or ignorant.

What are your obstacles?

What's keeping you from being happy and successful?

Is your job not important enough to work hard at it? Haven't we already put this myth to rest? There are no unimportant jobs, only workers who mistakenly believe that there are such jobs.

Are you not worthy of success? And where did you get that idea? Are you on the Forbes list of the most unworthy people in America? There's no such list! You're worthy!

Are there no opportunities for you? Have you even been looking for them? They are there, waiting for someone to "seize the opportunity." And listen, if you don't see any, you can always make your own.

Do you lack the education or experience that is needed to get ahead? What's stopping you from getting them? Money? There are all kinds of financial aid available for people who are looking for it. Time? There's no better time than now. Tell me something, in a few years from now, would you rather be where you want to be, or still be where you are right now, wishing you were somewhere else and wondering what might have been? There's an old Chinese proverb that says, "If we don't change the direction we're going, we're likely to end up where we're headed."

Are you not doing your best because you hate your job? Did you ever stop to think that if you did it better, you wouldn't hate it so much? Besides, aren't you being paid to do it, whether you hate it or not?

Do you think that your boss doesn't like you for some reason? If you're doing a good job, what reason could he have? And what if you were doing a good job, and he still didn't like you? Then he's an idiot, and if you let an idiot stand in your way, that makes you one too. Am I right?

Is your boss incompetent? Is that any reason not to do a good job? It seems to me that it would be a good reason to try even harder.

Is there something in your past, either at work or not, that is standing in your way? Don't you think you deserve a second chance? I think you do, and so will many other good people. Be honest about your past mistakes, and show how you've learned from them and changed for the better. Someone will give you a second chance. In any case, you won't know if you don't try.

Are there some co-workers who are "out to get you?" So what? Let them waste their time trying to get even while you're working on getting ahead. Don't worry about petty little people because they're only hurting themselves and they're not worth worrying about.

Is the competition at work too intense for you? Why be afraid of a little competition? It's good for you. Besides, you shouldn't be competing with others anyway; you should be competing with yourself. I guarantee that as you keep getting better and better, there won't be any real competition for you. You'll wish there was.

Are you handicapped (sorry, challenged), physically or mentally, or are you of the "wrong" gender, race, skin color, nationality, or sexual preference? Are you the victim of discrimination? Then, if you are, isn't it even more important that you do the best job you can do? If there is discrimination in the workplace, the best thing you can do is to demonstrate, by your words and deeds, that it is wrong, and that it has no place in the workplace, or anywhere for that matter. Many who are just like you did just that, and succeeded.

Are you afraid of failing? Is that why you're not even trying to succeed? Did you ever stop to think that because you're not trying, you will most definitely fail? Does that make any sense to you? And what if you do fail? Big deal. As a great fighter once said, "It's not how many times you get knocked down that counts, but how many times you get back up." Failure, you must understand, is not a final destination unless you decide to make it so; it's really just a temporary setback if you decide to move ahead. From each setback, you become better, stronger, and more knowledgeable. Sometimes, you have to fail in order to succeed. As Charles Kettering observed, "You will never stub your toe standing still. The faster you go, the more chance there is of stubbing your toe, but the more chance you have of getting somewhere."

Do you have personal problems that are consuming your time and energy? Have you asked for any help, and if not, why not? What are you waiting for, for your boss to notice that your work is now suffering because of your problem? How is that going to make things better? It seems to me that it will make things even worse.

Do you believe, perhaps, that you're unlucky? If it wasn't for bad luck, you'd have no luck at all, right? Who cares? Luck has nothing to do with real success. Only the people who fail believe that it does. The people who succeed know better.

Do you think you're too old? Well, according to the most powerful men and women in business today, you're not too old. Most people who succeed do so between the ages of forty to sixty, and sometimes well beyond. Their stories fill many books. Hey, I'm sixty four, and if I thought that I was too old, I would never have written this book. Now aren't you glad about that?

Do you think you're too young? Listen, kid, if you are young, be thankful for it. You have such an advantage over the rest of us old fogies. You have time to decide what you want to do with your life; you can choose any career, and devote years to being successful at it; with no family to support, you can take jobs at lower wages and work your way up to the top, getting valuable experience along the way; you can save small amounts of money every month, and through the magic of compounding, watch it grow rapidly as you get older; and best of all, you can form good work habits now, and not have to be burdened by bad habits throughout your working years. My advice to you is this—enjoy your youth, but not at the expense of the rest of your life. Spend some of the time you have now preparing for the times to come.

If you look closely at these obstacles, you will notice something of great significance—they are obstacles you put up yourself. They're what I like to call, "obstacle illusions," because they only exist in your mind. The good news is that you put them in your head, so you can also take them out. For most of them, if you just don't think of them as obstacles, they won't get in your way. Henry Ford once said, "Obstacles are those frightful things you see when you take your eyes off your goals." If you keep your eyes on achieving your goals and serving your purpose, there will be no obstacles that you can't overcome. Remember also, it's not the size of the obstacle that matters, but the size of your heart and the intensity of your resolve. Be strong, my friend, and never surrender.

SUMMARY

- There will be obstacles along your path to success.
- Almost all obstacles can be overcome with a little faith, hard work, persistence, creativity, and enthusiasm.
- Even if you can't overcome an obstacle, you can always become stronger for having tried.
- Most of the obstacles you will face will exist only in your mind.

Assignments:

1. Look at the obstacles that we talked about, and see if any of them describe the way you feel. Sit down and write out a plan to overcome them, and get to work ASAP on putting that plan into place.

Lesson Nineteen: Taking Action

Objectives:

1. To understand the difference between knowing and doing.
2. To act on what you know.

> This book, being about work, is, by its very nature, about violence—to the spirit as well as the body... It is about daily humiliations. To survive the day is triumph enough for the walking wounded among the great many of us.—Studs Terkel in Working, 1972

This book, *Working 101*, is not about violence, humiliation, or surviving the day. It's about being the best worker you can be, and doing a lot more than merely surviving. You deserve more; you deserve to be walking tall, not walking wounded. You're a hard working person, doing your best to make a living for yourself and for your family. You don't need someone telling you how miserable your life at work is; you need someone helping you to make it better.

That's why I wrote *Working 101*. It pains me to see so many of my fellow workers so miserable at their jobs, and it frustrates me to know that there's so little help available to them. Something had to be done. Somebody had to take a stand for the working class.

I've been working now for some fifty one years, ever since I was thirteen years old. (That makes me twenty nine if you're counting.) In those fifty one years, I have seen so many dissatisfied workers, and so much laziness, rudeness, ignorance, incompetence, selfishness, waste-fulness, carelessness, silliness, and indifference to fill a hundred books.

I've heard so much complaining about bosses and co-workers and customers and wages and benefits and everything else under the sun, that I sometimes wish that I could have been a psychiatrist, or better still, a bartender. At least then, I would have been paid to listen to all that sh...stuff, and maybe I would've gotten a few free drinks instead of having to spend my evenings after work having to pay for them at the corner pub.

It was twenty five years ago when I decided to write this book. I'm sorry that it has taken me this long to finish it, but I hope you have found the book to be well worth the wait.

There is no better time for this book than the present. The need for this information is well established, and in my humble opinion, *Working 101* is exactly what is needed. I believe it should be taught in every high school to all seniors, in all community colleges, and in all businesses to all new and current workers. And I know what you might be thinking—that I would believe that because it's my book.

It's not my book, it's yours, and you can think what you want, but I know in my heart that my intentions are good and my desire to help is sincere.

Enough about me, we're here to talk about you. You can't continue going to work, dreading the day; you can't continue going home after work, taking your frustrations out on your family and friends; you can't continue being miserable, and ending up as just another statistic, like the 26% of workers who feel emotionally drained by work, or the 36% who feel "used up" at the end of the day, or the 28% who have little or no energy left when they get home. (from a 1997 study by the Families and Work Institute.) You deserve better.

Putting your knowledge to work

You now have at your fingertips all the best information you will need to be a happy and successful worker. I have done for you all that I can. The rest is up to you. Now, you must take this information, and put it to good use. "Mere knowledge," said T.W.Palmer, "is not power, it is only possibility. Action is power; and its highest manifestation is when it is directed by knowledge." It's the combination of knowledge and action that leads to success.

Before you act, you should know how to act appropriately; knowing how to act, you must take action. There is a huge difference between knowing what has to be done, and doing what has to be done, especially when you're getting paid for what you do, and not for what you know.

"Nothing comes merely by thinking about it," as John Wanamaker said. Besides, how much thinking can you do? I mean, you can only sit on the toilet for so long. So, get up, flush the toilet, and take action. Take action especially if you're dissatisfied, but even if you're not. As Will Rogers commented, "Even if you're on the right track, you'll get run over if you just sit there."

Success, you must understand, is there for the taking. You've always had the ability to be successful, but you must reach out to take it—you must take the

Mike Jacobs

information from *Working 101*, and put it to good use;
you must take charge of your life, take control of your
thoughts, actions, and emotions, take pride in who you
are and what you do to make a living, and take the initiative to make things happen, to get things done, and
to change things for the better. You must remember, as
Sophocles said, that "Heaven never helps the man who
will not act."

Begin at the beginning

Are you feeling a bit overwhelmed at this point? I
know that I've given you a lot of information to think
about, but it's all information you need to have. You
shouldn't feel overwhelmed. As Calvin Coolidge said,
"You can't do everything at once, but you can, and must,
do something at once." Start anywhere; do something;
do anything you can do. If you want to get anything
done, the best way to do it is simply to begin.

I'll let you in on a little secret—once you begin,
once you start making choices and taking action, everything will start falling into place. Good choices will
beget good choices; good habits will beget good habits.
You'll be on your way on the road to success in no time.

At this point, I would wish you luck, but we both
know that luck has nothing to do with success. Instead,
I'll wish you good health and happiness, and all the success in the world. I thank you for letting me share my
thoughts and feelings, and for putting up with my stupid
jokes. (How do you think my wife feels?) I apologize if
I offended anyone, including any ladies out there who
may have been offended by my use of the male gender
throughout the book. I meant no disrespect. I'm just a

guy, and I can't help myself. Besides, "he" is a lot easier to spell than "she," and "he/she" just doesn't sound right to me. Of course, everything I said in the book applies to women the same as to men.

I'd like to leave you with a quote by Henry Giles. It says a great deal—

Man must work. That is certain as the sun. But he may work grudgingly, or he may work gratefully; he may work as a man, or he may work as a machine. There is no work so rude that he may not exalt it; no work so impassive, that he may not breathe a soul into it; no work so dull, that he may not enliven it.

SUMMARY

- There is a huge difference between knowing what has to be done and actually doing it.
- You're paid to get things done, but it helps to know what you're doing.
- You can be happy and successful at work.
- You deserve to be happy and successful at work.
- It's your choice—you can be happy and successful, or you can be miserable.

Assignments:

1. Read the book again.
2. This time, do the assignments, and don't make me have to tell you again.
3. Have some fun, but take this seriously.
4. Check the obituaries. If you're not listed, go to work.

5. At work, take action on the information from the book.
6. Be happy and be successful.
7. Keep in touch. See the Appendix on how to reach me.

Appendix:
Continuing to Learn
(A Working Bibliography)

Although *Working 101* contains a wealth of information, it is far from being all the information you
will ever need. You can always learn more, and there
is always more to be learned. Information, like everything else, changes. The best information today may not
be the best information tomorrow. It may no longer be
accurate, relevant, timely, or sufficient.

You must continue to learn if you are to become
successful and stay successful. You must develop a thirst
for knowledge, but for knowledge that can be used to
make you a better worker.

I'd like to help you to do this. I'm going to give you
the names of some of the books and websites I used in
writing this book, but I also want you to stay in touch with
me. You can write to me in care of the publisher, visit
my website at www.working101book.com, or send me
an e-mail at Mikejacobs101@aol.com. On the website,
you'll find lots of helpful and humorous information,
learn about other services we offer (including seminars),
and have an opportunity to share your experiences with
others. I will gladly answer any and all of your questions.

The bibliography that follows is presented in a
little different format from the usual bibliography. I've
listed books by categories, added some notes in paren-
theses briefly describing what the books are about, and
put an asterisk next to the books I highly recommend.

Websites

Families and Work Institute
http://www.familiesandwork.org

Bureau of Labor Statistics
http://www.bls.gov

U.S. Department of Labor
http://www.dol.gov

Books on motivation and personal growth

Chopra, Deepak. *The Seven Spiritual Laws of Success.* San Rafael, CA: New World Library, 1994.

Covey, Steven R. *The 7 Habits of Highly Effective People.* New York: Fireside/Simon & Schuster, 1989.

Hill, Napoleon. *Think and Grow Rich. New York:* Ballantine Books, 1960.*

Mandino, Og. *The Greatest Salesman in the World.* (Part II). New York: Bantam Books, 1988.

Snow, Patrick. *Creating Your Own Destiny: How to Get Exactly What You Want Out of Life and Work.* Hoboken, N.J.: John Wiley and Sons, 2010. (Both of Patrick's books are great for those who want to rise above working for someone else to start their own businesses. Highly motivating.)

Snow, Patrick. *The Affluent Entrepreneur: 20 Proven Principles for Achieving Prosperity.* Hoboken, N.J.: John Wiley and Sons, 2011.

Books on living

Brown, Jr. H. Jackson. *A Father's Book of Wisdom.* Nashville, TN: Rutledge Hill Press, 1988. (Quotations)

O'Reilly, Bill. *Who's Looking Out For You?* New York: Broadway Books, 2003.*

Books on managing time and stress

Cooper, Cary L. *The Stress Check.* Prentice Hall, NJ: Spectrum Books, 1981.

Le Boeuf, Michael. *Working Smart.* New York: Warner Books, 1979. (Time)

Books on business and working

Byham, William C. & Cox, Jeff. *Heroz.* New York: Fawcett Columbine, 1994. (Empowerment)

Byham, William C. & Cox, Jeff. *Zapp! The Lightning of Empowerment.* New York: Harmony Books, 1988. (Teamwork)

Cherrington, David. *The Work Ethic: Working Values and Values that Work.* New York: Amacom, 1980.

Gallagher Hately, B.J. & Schmidt, Warren H. *A Peacock in the Land of Penguins.* San Francisco, CA: Berrett-Koehler Publishers, 1995. (A story about fitting in when you're different)

Gallwey, W. Timothy. *The Inner Game of Work.* New York, Random House, 2000.

Herzberg, Fredrick. *Motivation to Work.* New York: John Wiley & Sons, 1959 (revised 1993.)

Johnson, Spencer, M.D. *Who Moved My Cheese?* New York: G.P. Putnam's Sons, 1998. (A story about change.)

Kelley, Robert E. *How To Be A Star At Work. New York:* Times Business, 1998.

Lane, Fredrick S. *The Naked Employee: How Technology Is Compromising Workplace Privacy.* New York: Amacom, 2003. (FYI, there are no naked pictures in this book, hence no asterisk.)

Lundin, Stephen C. *Fish.* New York: Hyperion, 1996. * (Customer service, and there are several books in the Fish series)

Maxwell, John C. *The 17 Undisputable Laws of Teamwork.* Nashville, TN: Thomas Nelson Publishers, 2003.

McCord, Robert. *The Best Advice Ever For Becoming A Success At Work.* Kansas City, MO: McMeel Publishers, 2001. (Quotations, but not the best advice. That honor belongs to *Working 101,* if you ask me.)

Roberts, Wess. PhD. *Leadership Secrets of Attila The Hun.* New York: Warner Books, 1985. *
Rosner, Bob. *Working Wounded.* New York: Warner Books, 1998.

Terkel, Studs. *Working.* New York: Ballantine Books, 1972. * (stories about hard working men and women.)

And there is so much more information out there. You can find it in bookstores, in libraries, and online. You can read, you can take courses, and, of course, you can always contact me. I'll leave you with this thought— the smartest workers are not the ones who think they know everything and do nothing to learn more, but the ones who know that they don't know everything and continue to learn.

***